EXPOSING

THE SPIRIT OF MAMMON

ENDORSEMENTS

As followers of Jesus, one of the quickest things that can get us off track from the plans and purposes of God is the spirit of mammon. That's why Ashley Terradez's book *Exposing the Spirit of Mammon* is a critical read for today. It dives deeply into what the Bible says about money and how we can apply these timeless truths to our modern era. I've known and worked alongside Ashley for over a decade, and I can say with confidence that he is a man who practices what he preaches. If you want to learn from someone who walks in the blessings of God with integrity and generosity, this is your book. You will be encouraged to trust God with your finances and receive His blessings in a powerful new way!

BILLY EPPERHART
CEO Andrew Wommack Minsistries & Charis Bible College
Founder & President of WealthBuilders Inc & Tricord Global

Our culture is bewitched with the westernized notion of being rich at all costs or a mentality that preaches grind until you become wealthy. The celebration of greed and selfishness has sadly risen to a place of normalcy. Not only is this prevalent in the world's system of operation, but it has infiltrated many of the church's pulpits! It has truly become one of the great deceptions of our time.

In his new book *Exposing the Spirit of Mammon*, my friend Ashley Terradez offers a counter strike of long overdue biblical truth. He counters the onslaught of selfishness brought about by the love of money. When reading every page of this book, I found myself experiencing internal joy from the heart of God! My friend Ashley has pointed out the tragedy of exchanging what God has provided for a dangerous counterfeit! God offers His blessing, while the system of this world offers its seductive false replica—mammon.

You are about to discover that mammon is far more than money—it is a demon spirit that drives the love of money!

In this excellent book, *Exposing the Spirit of Mammon*, you'll learn what mammon really is but, most importantly, how to break its hold! Ashley will take you on an imperative journey that will lay out the tools and necessary revelation to escape mammon's seductive trap.

Prepare to break free and experience biblical abundance and God's increase! You are about to exchange the counterfeit for the real and see the spirit of mammon cast out of your life forever!

JOSEPH Z
Author, Broadcaster, Prophetic Voice
JosephZ.Com

The apostle Paul prophetically warned that society at the end of the age would become self-consumed and populated with those who were chiefly loyal to themselves—those whose lives would be consequently and fundamentally lopsided and off-center. This lets us know that a last-days society will be so self-fixated that it will extravagantly sacrifice at the altar of self.

Because you and I are the ones living in that society at the end of this age, we need to be careful about self-absorption and being ruled by the spirit of mammon. Like it or not, at some point, we have all veered off track into selfishness and have made mistakes with money and other resources. To help us stay spiritually on track, it is healthy to periodically do a self-examination and allow the Holy Spirit to search our hearts to show us if self is too highly exalted in our lives.

I am certain that Ashley Terradez's book *Exposing the Spirit of Mammon* will be used by the Spirit of God to help many make such an examination to keep their heart in a right condition regarding self—to keep selfishness at bay and to use their money and other resources as God would have them do.

God is avidly in favor of His people being blessed with money and material possessions—unless those things leave our hands and enter our hearts! That is what happens when the spirit of mammon is in control. But as Ashley so marvelously states in the first chapter of his book, money is a lousy master! Those who allow money to become their master inevitably reap disastrous consequences in their lives—in their families and their businesses, ministries, or organizations. You see, money was never meant to be a master; it was meant to be an instrument.

Today I heartily recommend Ashley's book *Exposing the Spirit of Mammon*. If you already own it, I encourage you to start reading it—and if you haven't gotten a copy of it yet, get one today! This is a book the Holy Spirit will use to strengthen and reinforce your heart to stay on the right path where it pertains to this critical subject of mammon!

RICK RENNER
Minister, Author, Broadcaster
Moscow, Russia

I thank God that He has put people like Ashley Terradez in the Body of Christ and given them insight, revelation, and the ability to make clear what the Bible says about money, material wealth, and financial prosperity. *Exposing the Spirit of Mammon* is a message for every believer and one that will shine a light, revealing the hidden motives of the heart, and enable the reader to make the necessary changes, unlocking unlimited potential for growth and increase.

JEREMY PEARSONS
Pastor of Legacy Church
Green Mountain Falls, Colorado

I'm so grateful for the teaching of my friend Ashley Terradez. He presents the Word of God in such a way that we can grasp the truth and apply it immediately.

I highly encourage you to get a hold of the wisdom Ashley reveals in his new book, *Exposing the Spirit of Mammon*. He brings clarity as to why people may feel "stuck" in their finances. Ashley powerfully exposes mammon's lies and encourages believes to heed the voice of their Good Shepherd. As believers, grabbing hold of the revelation in this book will transform the way we deal with and think about finances. Thank you, Ashley, for bringing such powerful truth from the Word of God that leaves a lasting impact!

JOEL HUIZING
Lead Pastor of Impact Life Church
Red Deer, Canada
President of Impacting Canada Ministries

You were made to prosper ... the Gospel is prosperity! The voice of Mammon comes to steal that promise and distract us from the call and purpose God has for our everyday lives. Ashley Terradez's latest book, *Exposing the Spirit of Mammon,* clearly defines God's voice and the voice of mammon. Understanding these two voices is pivotal in your journey to understanding how to pursue the Father and His heart for your life, while rejecting the enemy's voice through the spirit of mammon. Mammon is indeed a cunning voice: "Did God really say," "Are you sure you can give that much," or "Did God really call you here?"

Whether you are a young entrepreneur, seasoned business owner, pastor, or leader, *Exposing the Spirit of Mammon* is a must-read to discern the carnal voice of the enemy and tune your ear to the still small whisper of your Father's voice. Faith and freedom abound as you break free and enter into the next chapter of your journey with Jesus!

Jeff VanderWal
CEO of ClearShift
Host of Built for a Purpose Podcast
actlife.ca

EXPOSING
THE SPIRIT OF MAMMON

MAKE GOD NOT MONEY YOUR MASTER

ASHLEY TERRADEZ

Published by Harrison House Publishers
Shippensburg, PA 17257

ISBN 13 TP: 978-1-6675-0418-6
ISBN 13 eBook: 978-1-6675-0419-3

For Worldwide Distribution, Printed in the U.S.A.
1 2 3 4 5 6 7 8 / 28 27 26 25 24

CONTENT

FOREWORD

I was probably 25 years old—just starting out in itinerate preaching ministry. I would travel and minister domestically, hoping to raise funds for my international evangelistic work. I was full of faith and sure that God had called me. My confidence was such that I would tell pastors who had invited me to preach that if they allowed me to share my vision and take up an offering, I would pay for the rest. I was willing to take 100 percent of the financial risk. The plane tickets, the hotel rooms, rental cars, food—I trusted God to take care of it all, plus the massive expenses of international evangelistic campaigns and the support of my little family at home. I just knew that when people saw the fire in my eyes and heard the passion in my voice, they would recognize the urgency of the hour, know that God had sent me, and support my work generously.

For the most part, I was right. So many people stood to help this young upstart preacher, and I experienced one miracle after another. The finances were tight, but God never failed me.

Then I received an invitation to preach at a church in Pennsylvania. I accepted the invitation and journeyed from Florida, where I lived, full of faith.

Our prior arrangement notwithstanding, during the worship, the pastor turned to me and said, "Son, I've decided that instead of taking an offering for you, the church is just going to bless you out of our general fund." Such a departure from our agreement could only mean he was planning to give more than an offering would collect. I preached my heart out and ministered to the people in the altars. As I left, the pastor handed me a plain white envelope and thanked me for my ministry. I waited until I reached my rental car in the parking lot to see what was inside.

As I pulled out the check, my heart sank. It was a paltry $150. It wouldn't even pay for one leg of my plane ticket. I was trying to raise $30K for my evangelistic work, but now I was not even sure if I could put food on the table.

It might seem dramatic now, but I felt utterly and completely overwhelmed for a twenty-five-year-old with very few resources and more than my share of responsibility. In fact, I felt like I was suffocating—like a python was tightening around my chest. Each breath seemed more difficult than the last. My mind began to race. What could I cut? How could I shift things around to make ends meet?

Suddenly, the Holy Spirit touched me, and I had a moment of clarity. I realized what was happening. I had allowed the enemy to move me from a position of faith to fear. Now I was in the flesh. I was in survival mode. And my knee-jerk reaction was to contract, to squeeze every last penny I had in stingy, self-preservation. Some people, driven by greed and materialism, bow to the spirit of mammon in worship. But I was bowing to mammon in fear. My motives were different, but my posture was the same. I was allowing that suffocating spirit to intimidate and cow me.

When the Holy Spirit opened my eyes to it, I was filled with holy anger, not at the pastor, but at that suffocating mammon spirit. I knew I had to do something. I felt like If I allowed that thing to tighten its grip on my faith, I would live in poverty and fear. I had to break free, and I had to do it fast!

My reaction was unsophisticated and unpolished, awkward even, but it was authentic. I got out of the car, walked back into the church, found the pastor, and invited him, his family, and their pastoral team out to lunch at my own expense at the most excellent restaurant in town. As I paid the bill, I knew I was literally spending the last little bit of money I had. But I felt elated. My reckless generosity was an act of protest against the devil. The Lord provided for all my needs and even paid for my evangelistic campaign. But best of all, I had refused to bow to mammon!

That experience was a defining moment for me. The Lord helped me recognize and resist the spirit of mammon. It was a life-changing revelation. In a similar way, I believe that the book you hold in your hands will be a defining moment for you!

In *Exposing the Spirit of Mammon*, Ashley Terradez reminds us of a fundamental spiritual truth: we cannot serve God and mammon. This truth is not merely a piece of advice but a profound spiritual principle that can shape our lives and determine our destiny. The spirit of mammon is actively working to draw us away from the Lord. It seeks to become our master, exerting control over our thoughts, decisions, and priorities. But the good news is that you can be equipped with the knowledge and authority to resist its influence and take power over it in Jesus' name!

As you exercise this authority, you shift the balance of power in your life. Mammon loses its hold, and God's dominion becomes more evident. Your heart and mind become aligned with the will of God, and you begin to make financial decisions that honor Him.

But remember, authority is not merely about issuing commands but also about taking responsibility. We must be good stewards of the resources and finances that God entrusts to us. In doing so, we demonstrate our faithfulness and reliability as servants of the Lord.

This book will equip you with the knowledge and understanding needed to exercise this authority effectively. As you read and absorb Ashley's principles, you will grow in spiritual discernment. You will recognize the deceptive tactics of mammon and be able to confront them head-on.

Additionally, you will discover that money is a neutral tool, waiting to be directed by your Holy Spirit-led choices. Rather than allowing money to dictate your decisions, you will learn to make it your servant. You will use it for good, supporting God's work, blessing others, and meeting your needs with wisdom and stewardship.

Ashley Terradez is a dear friend and a dedicated servant of the Lord. His deep understanding of spiritual principles and commitment to teaching the Word of God shine through on every page of this book. Ashley's work is not merely the result of intellectual study; it is the fruit of a life lived in communion with God, marked by unwavering faith and a passion for sharing the truth.

In *Exposing the Spirit of Mammon*, Ashley Terradez delves into the timeless battle between pursuing wealth and pursuing God's Kingdom. He draws from both Scripture and personal experiences to reveal the insidious tactics of the spirit of mammon, a force that has ensnared many throughout history, even the devil himself.

As we journey through these pages, Ashley masterfully uncovers the age-old strategies that have lured countless individuals into the trap of serving money rather than God. He reminds us that we cannot serve two masters, and he equips us with the knowledge and wisdom needed to discern mammon's voice and reclaim our rightful position with God as our ultimate Master.

One of Ashley's most profound insights is the distinction between money as a tool and money as a master. Money is neither inherently good nor evil; instead, it is a neutral resource that can be used for various purposes. Through Ashley's teachings, you will understand that money is meant to serve you as you faithfully serve the Lord.

In our materialistic world, it is easy to become distracted by pursuing earthly wealth, forgetting our true identity as spiritual beings. Ashley reminds us that we are children of the Most High God, citizens of a heavenly kingdom and recipients of spiritual blessings that far surpass the temporary allure of material possessions.

Exposing the Spirit of Mammon is more than just a book; it is a road map to a transformed financial mindset and a renewed commitment to serving God above all else. As you embark on this journey of revelation and empowerment through Ashley Terradez's teachings, may you grow closer to God, confidently wielding the keys of authority and living a life that glorifies your heavenly Father in all you do.

DANIEL KOLENDA
President of Christ for all Nations
Lead Pastor of Nations Church

SPECIAL MESSAGE

I believe one of the biggest problems in the body of Christ today is an inability to discern spiritual things. The vast majority of Christians are what the Bible calls "carnal." Carnal doesn't only describe those who hate God but there are millions of very nice, moral, carnal Christians.

Carnality is simply being dominated by or limited to our five senses. There is so much more to reality than what we can see, taste, hear, smell, or feel. There is a whole spiritual realm that exists which we can't see, but it's real. In fact, the spiritual realm is more real than this physical realm. The spiritual realm created this physical realm. It's the parent force.

A lack of understanding this is one of the biggest hinderances when it comes to money.

Money, and our ability to get it, is not only a physical thing. It's the Lord who gives us power to get wealth, and there is a demonic spirit that is constantly at work to use the love of money to make our lives miserable. Unless a person receives a revelation from the Lord on this, that spirit of mammon will control us. True prosperity is spiritual.

I've known Ashley and his whole family since we first met in England in 2005. They graduated from our UK Charis Bible College and then came to the US and did a third year at our Woodland Park Colorado Charis campus. Both Ashley and

Carlie worked for me for over a decade until they went out on their own to spread the good news gospel.

I got to know Ashley up close and can verify that Ashley has dealt with this spirit of mammon. He is a radical giver and a radical receiver. As one of his board members, I've seen their ministry finances increase supernaturally and it is directly related to the truths Ashley shares in this book. Ashley and Carlie have seen miraculous provision in their personal and ministry life, and you can, too.

Money is a tool the Lord gives us to use for His glory. But mammon seeks to make money our master, and it's a cruel master. One of the biggest problems in marriage, and life in general, is financial pressures. Until you break free of this spirit of mammon, you will never find the peace God wants you to have and you certainly won't be able to accomplish what He has called you to do. It takes money to live.

There is an anointing on the Terradez's lives and ministry in this area of finances. They are not sharing theory with you. This is revelation from the Lord and it's working in their lives. Ashley exposes this spirit of mammon so clearly that it will change the way you deal with money. You will become the master and money will be your servant.

I recommend Ashley's teaching without reservation and assure you that God is no respecter of persons. What the Lord has done for Ashley and Carlie, He will do for you. Get ready to be set free from the fear of lack and start enjoying the true Biblical prosperity the Lord wants you to have.

ANDREW WOMMACK
President and Founder of Charis Bible College
and Andrew Wommack Ministries
awmi.net

There is a very popular phrase that gets tossed around in Christian circles: "We are in the world, but we are not of it." This phrase itself is found nowhere in Scripture but is a true conclusion drawn from various verses.

> We know [positively] that we are of God, and the whole world [around us] is under the power of the evil one.
>
> 1 John 5:19 AMPC

In the Garden of Gethsemane, the night before His crucifixion, Jesus prayed, *"Now I am no longer in the world, but these [Jesus' followers] are in the world..."* (John 17:11). It seems a bit obvious, but you and I *do* live in the physical world.

Jesus then also prayed, *"I have given them Your word; and the world has hated them because they are not of the world, just as I am not of the world. I do not pray that You should take them out of the world, but that You should keep them from the evil one. They are not of the world, just as I am not of the world"* (John 17:14-16).

So here in John 17, we see that Jesus said we are living in the world, yet we are not "of" the world. But what does this mean, and how does it affect our daily lives?

Although we are spiritual beings, we live in a physical world. We live according to spiritual laws of the Kingdom of God, but we still have to deal with the natural world in which we live.

Everything we do in this world requires money: buying or renting a home, transportation, food, electricity, education, etc. We make financial transactions every day, just like those who are not of the Kingdom of God.

The problem is, Christians forget that although we are living physical lives within a natural world, we interact with it from a spiritual perspective, according to spiritual laws.

For example, even an unbeliever realizes that in order to meet their financial needs, they need to work a job, invest, set aside the money needed for vacations, and save for retirement. Although believers will understand they need to take the same wise financial steps, they know there is an unseen variable working on their behalf as part of a spiritual Kingdom: the blessing and favor of God!

> And you shall remember the Lord your God, for it is He who gives you power to get wealth, that He may establish His covenant which He swore to your fathers, as it is this day.
>
> Deuteronomy 8:18

There are spiritual benefits to being of the Kingdom of God, rather than the kingdom of the world, but there are also spiritual forces that are working against us. Our enemy, the devil, does not *want* the children of God to fully experience the blessing and favor He has made available to us. And he has devised deceptions that will cause confusion and short-circuit the good things God has in store.

The most common deception the enemy has planted in this world, as part of the world's system itself, is the work of the spirit of mammon. The goal of the spirit of mammon is to get us to serve *it* rather than the Lord.

> No one can serve two masters; for either he will hate the one and love the other, or else he will be loyal to the one and despise the other. You cannot serve God and mammon.
>
> Matthew 6:24.

Mammon is not just money. It is the spirit *behind* money. Money in itself is not evil, but it is the *love* of money which is the root of evil (1 Timothy 6:10). To escape the trap of serving mammon, we must understand how to trust the Lord fully in the area of finances.

Years ago, my kids wanted a dog. At the time, we lived in the mountains and shared the land around us with bears, and most likely a mountain lion or two. Now, there are two options for dogs when you live in the country: either get a big dog who can give a bear or mountain lion a run for its money, or a small dog you can use as a decoy!

To spare my family the trauma associated with option two, we went with option one and got a Chesapeake Bay Retriever. Although he would grow to be a larger dog, he was a very cute puppy!

One day, the puppy got ahold of a chicken bone, and my wife, Carlie, said, "Get that—he'll choke!"

I went to get the bone and said, "Hey, puppy, give that to me." But when I reached for it, that cute little puppy turned into a mini Cujo—he went after me with a vengeance!

After that, I was intimidated by my own little puppy! It's embarrassing to be scared of your own little dog.

So, I asked someone experienced with dogs, and he said, "Dogs are either being led, or they are leading. There is no middle ground. Your dog is either leading you, or you are leading your dog. By default, your dog will be the leader."

That's why you can see even little dogs pulling their much larger owners down the street. Even little dogs can be scary and intimidating if they are not being led by their humans. The human must assert alpha dominance over the dog to ensure submissiveness.

Our finances are the same way! If you've never thought about leading your finances, your finances are leading you by default. There is no middle ground with money: you are either leading your money, or money is leading you. You are either serving God with your finances, or the spirit of mammon is deceiving you into serving it instead.

You might think, *Well, Ashley, I don't have any money!* It doesn't matter whether you have money or not, whether you are in debt, out of debt, broke or have millions in the bank.

Mammon is the voice of money, and if the voice of money is speaking to you—and you are listening to it—then it is leading you instead of you leading it.

Mammon can be incredibly subtle. It can convince you that your decisions are simply being wise. Sometimes the spirit of mammon can even cause you to spend money on things you wouldn't if you were being led by God rather than by the world.

As you continue reading, this book will continue exposing the spirit of mammon so you do not fall prey to its deceptions. At the end of the day, we need to get to the point where we are listening to the voice of God rather than the voice of mammon. If we want to fully experience the abundant life Jesus came to give us, we must obey the voice of God only and cannot let the voice of mammon lead us.

1

MONEY IS A LOUSY MASTER

Money is a huge part of how our world functions. We need it to buy food, clothes, a roof over our heads, transportation, communication, let alone recreational activities! Even if all you do is sit at home all day, money is still required just to survive. It's an unescapable part of life.

However, money makes a lousy master!

Most of us wouldn't think that money is our "master," would we? After all, money is a collection of inanimate objects. Dollar bills and coins, or digital numbers on a paycheck, direct deposits, and bank statements. How can such a thing be our master?

Whenever we make decisions in life, our default process is, "Can I afford this?" Whether it's deciding to buy a house, buy new clothes, go out to eat, or just get a cup of coffee, our bank account speaks to us.

Another way money can be our master is when we allow it to affect our emotions. Worry about how to pay our bills, playing the lottery or gambling in hope of a big win, or even being jealous of others' success—these are all ways we allow money to be our master.

The effects that money can have on us are natural symptoms of a spiritual cause. Remember, the spirit of mammon is the voice of money. It is a mask of the enemy that he uses to cause havoc in our lives.

When we allow mammon to be our master, it will cause us to make mistakes. We will make decisions that may look right from a natural perspective, but we will miss out on things the Lord is trying to tell us. God may sometimes tell us to do things that don't make financial sense in the natural; but if we are listening to the voice of mammon, we may end up in a position the Lord never intended for us.

The True Purpose of Money

No matter how we look at things—from either a natural or spiritual perspective—money has a purpose. We need it to survive in this world, but mere survival and financial success is not its true purpose.

Money is neither good nor evil. Ethically, money is completely neutral. It only has morality based on the actions taken by the hands who wield it. For example, let's say I give $100 to five different people. That money will adopt the integrity by which those people use it.

Maybe one person uses the $100 to buy drugs. Another buys a new pair of headphones. Perhaps the third gives all of it to their church, while the fourth takes their friends out to a bar. The fifth could just bury it in their backyard!

The point is, the $100 has no intrinsic morality: it is neither good nor evil. What it is used for, however, can have an infinite variety of results.

Money makes a lousy master, but it makes a great servant. Money is meant to be our servant, our slave. It is simply a *tool*. It can be used for so much good, especially when it comes to spreading the message of the Gospel to the world. When we use money rightly, we can do great things with it!

However, if we don't understand the *purpose* of why God wants us to be blessed in our finances, we will become self-centered, only looking to fulfill our own fleshly desires. The devil takes great advantage of that weakness. The spirit of mammon speaks to us to view money as evil, to desire wealth out of greed, or use money to control our life decisions. At best, it will cause us to use our finances for neutral purposes, and at worst, for evil.

My dad was a specialist in repairing cars, sometimes very expensive cars. He had many professional tools for the job. He'd take out his tools and oil them to prepare them for work. He then used the differently shaped tools to carefully tap out panels by hand so they could be repainted to look brand-new.

One day, I took Dad's hammers out and started beating on rocks. My dad was *not* pleased with me! It wasn't because he loved his hammers, but they were tools he needed to do his job. He loved what those tools could be used for—what they could achieve.

Money is the same way. It is a tool that can be used to accomplish powerful goals for the Kingdom of God! It costs money to put on conferences, to have people answer prayer lines, to travel for ministry, to broadcast on television—simply put, it costs money to spread the Gospel.

It costs money to open homes for children or shelters for abused women. Money is necessary to provide food, clothing, and shelter for those who need it. Financial resources are needed for nearly any project that is good and intended to help people!

Think of the story of the Good Samaritan in more modern terms. He picked up the beaten Jewish man in his nice car, drove him to a Hilton, and used his American Express card to pay for his housing and medical treatment! When you have the money, you have the tools you need to accomplish the good God directs you to do.

But money can also easily be misused. That is why Jesus made such a big deal about deciding who you will serve: God or money (Matthew 6:24). Serving both is impossible.

Money Talks

...money answers everything.

Ecclesiastes 10:19

The word *answers* here in Ecclesiastes 10:19 is the Hebrew word *anah,* which literally means to answer or respond. Money talks! It speaks to us. Money has an opinion on everything! Every time we make a decision, money is talking to us. Usually, the opinion of money—of mammon—is not the voice we should be following.

The spirit of mammon is the enemy's way of getting us to trust in something other than God.

Trust in the Lord with all your heart, and lean not on your own understanding; in all your ways acknowl-edge Him, and He shall direct your paths.

Proverbs 3:5-6

These two verses tell us that we are to trust in the Lord in everything in our lives. In every choice, our trust needs to be in Him, not in anything else, including our finances. The enemy, however, will use any tactic he can to draw our trust and atten-tion away from the Lord.

One of the enemy's main deceptions is to use the spirit of mammon—the voice of money—as a physical alternative to trusting in God. He knows that our success in this life is dependent upon our faith in the Lord and that if he can get us to trust in the things of the world instead, he can win. We can trust in money, pursue money, and be lured by money for the very things God has already freely provided to us!

Three Tricks

However, the devil doesn't have any new tricks. He uses the same strategies for deception and distraction that he has always used from the beginning. First John describes what the voice of mammon sounds like:

> *For all that is in the world—the lust of the flesh, the lust of the eyes, and the pride of life—is not of the Father, but is of the world.*
>
> 1 John 2:16

Each temptation we face in life can fit into one of these three categories: 1) the lust of the flesh; 2) the lust of the eyes; and 3) the pride of life. These tricks of the enemy are what he uses to distract us, to get our eyes off of Jesus and onto the world. They deceive us into living according to the natural principles of the world rather than the supernatural principles of the Word.

The devil doesn't have any new tricks—ways to trap us— and once we can spot them, we can avoid his traps. There are three times in the Word of God these strategies of the enemy are discussed in a way where we can see a clear connection between them.

The first was the original temptation of Eve in the garden of Eden. The second was the temptation of Jesus right before He began His earthly ministry. And the third is found in Mark 4, when Jesus was teaching the Parable of the Sower.

The Bible records the very first temptation of mankind in Genesis chapter 3. First, the enemy got Eve to question God's Word. Then came the temptation:

> *So when the woman saw that the tree was good for food, that it was pleasant to the eyes, and a tree desirable to make one wise, she took of its fruit and ate....*
>
> Genesis 3:6

When we look closely at what these words in the original Hebrew mean, the correlation with 1 John 2:16 becomes very clear.

The word *pleasant* is *taavah*, which means a desire. When it says "wise," it is the Hebrew word *sakal,* which means to be prudent. However, when you look closely at its usage, it means to "consider, instruct, prosper, deal prudently, have good success, [and] teach."

So, first Eve saw that the tree was good for food: this is the lust of the flesh. Second, she saw that it was desirable: this is the lust of the eyes. Third, she saw that it could make them wise, which would lead to success: that is the pride of life.

Isn't it interesting how these three tricks of the enemy, these temptations and traps, align so perfectly with 1 John 2:16?

Jesus was tempted in this very same way:

> *And the devil said to Him, "If You are the Son of God, command this stone to become bread."*
>
> Luke 4:3

> *Then the devil, taking Him up on a high mountain, showed Him all the kingdoms of the world in a moment of time. And the devil said to Him, "All this*

authority I will give You, and their glory; for this has been delivered to me, and I give it to whomever I wish. Therefore, if You will worship before me, all will be Yours."

Luke 4:5-7

Then he brought Him to Jerusalem, set Him on the pinnacle of the temple, and said to Him, "If You are the Son of God, throw Yourself down from here. For it is written: 'He shall give His angels charge over you, To keep you,' and, 'In their hands they shall bear you up, Lest you dash your foot against a stone.'"

Luke 4:9-11

In Luke 4:2, it says Jesus was hungry. That lust of the flesh was probably very hard to deny, but He did! The devil then promised Jesus ultimate power and success. This temptation was the lust of the eyes, as the devil showed Jesus everything he would give Him if He would just deny His Father in heaven.

Then came the third temptation regarding the pride of life. How prideful would it be for a person to throw himself from a building and expect angels to catch him?

Later, Jesus taught a parable to expose the dangers of putting our trust in the voice of mammon rather than in the Word of God.

In Mark 4, Jesus tells a parable of how the Word of God can be stripped of its power in our lives. This is a large passage that deals with many things, but one specific portion corresponds with these three main categories of temptation, which the enemy still uses to deceive us today.

Now these are the ones sown among thorns; they are the ones who hear the word, and the cares of this world, the deceitfulness of riches, and the desires for other things entering in choke the word, and it becomes unfruitful.

Mark 4:18-19

Here we see Jesus listing the same temptations that the enemy has placed in front of us since the beginning: the lust of the flesh (desires for other things); the lust of the eyes (deceitfulness of riches); and the pride of life (the cares of this world).

These are the things that can choke the Word in our lives. We hear the Word, believe in the goodness of God, that all of His promises are "yes" and "amen." Yet we still experience poverty, anxiety, and sickness!

When we follow the voice of mammon—and fall into these traps—they enter in and choke the Word, and it becomes unfruitful.

If you have heard the Word, believed it, and planted it in your life, but it hasn't born fruit, it is because the voice of mammon—the cares of this world, the deceitfulness of riches and the lust for other things—has been speaking to you, distracting you, and therefore choked the Word in your heart.

If you don't see the Word of God working in your life, go back and see where you've been distracted by these other things, by mammon. It's not about money at all. It's about when you've listened to the voice of mammon over the voice—the Word—of God.

2

THE LUST OF THE FLESH

The most obvious trick of the enemy is when the voice of mammon speaks to us through the lust of our flesh. When we think of sin, most often it falls into this category. From sexual sin to gluttony, we associate most sin with the lust of the flesh. This is essentially referring to anything that gratifies something our bodies desire according to our five senses: taste, touch, smell, sight, and hearing.

Let's look again at how the Amplified Version, Classic Edition clarifies the lust of the flesh:

> For all that is in the world—the lust of the flesh [craving for sensual gratification]....
>
> 1 John 2:16

This voice tells us that we are missing out! At the very basic level, we want something in our flesh that our bodies will enjoy. We ignore the fruit of the Spirit we have been given—self-control—and give in to the temptation.

This can take so many different forms, as all of us tend to be tempted more strongly by different things. One person may have a sweet tooth that just will not be denied, whereas another finds themselves addicted to inappropriate movies or television shows.

Perhaps it is sexual perversion that screams, "If you don't do this, you are missing out on something amazing!" Or drugs that will bring you a physical high, a sensation you can't seem to find anywhere else. Mammon cries out to you, "Nothing else will satisfy you. Nothing else will make you feel this good."

> Let no one say when he is tempted, "I am tempted by God"; for God cannot be tempted by evil, nor does He Himself tempt anyone. But each one is tempted when he is drawn away by his own desires and enticed.
>
> James 1:13-14

Now, don't misunderstand this verse: when you are born again, your spirit desires nothing but good! You become a new creature, old things pass away, and you become new (2 Corinthians 5:17)! These desires that entice us via the lust of the flesh come from just that: the flesh. Our bodies are the ones who are in rebellion through our natural five senses.

It's important for you to understand before we move on that even though the voice of mammon may try to tempt you into satisfying the desires of the flesh, God has given you the grace, the power, the ability to be free! Sin has no power over you anymore.

> And having been set free from sin, you became slaves of righteousness.
>
> Romans 6:18

Good for Food

The lust of the flesh can be found front and center in the story of Eve's temptation. After the devil had performed his fear-of-missing-out and God-is-holding-out-on-you tricks, the basic motives of the flesh kicked in. Eve looked at the fruit growing on the tree of the knowledge of good and evil and *"saw that the tree was good for food"* (Genesis 3:6).

It looked good! Have you ever seen a dessert that just made your mouth water? That's what was happening here. I imagine Eve took a glance and thought, *Man, that looks delicious! I bet it will taste amazing. I wonder if it tastes even better than all the other fruit God has provided for me?*

Her fleshly desire to taste something yummy tempted her into eating! Isn't that sad? It just highlights the importance of understanding that just because your flesh wants something that will bring sensual gratification, it doesn't mean it will be good for you. Yes, we all know this on a surface level, but we must renew our minds to our righteousness in Christ so that temptations of the flesh cannot rule over us, control our decisions.

Jesus was tempted in the very same way.

And Jesus, being filled with the Holy Spirit, returned from the Jordan and was led by the Spirit into the wilderness, being tempted for forty days by the devil. And in those days He ate nothing, and afterward, when they had ended, He was hungry. And the devil said to Him, "If You are the Son of God, command this stone to become bread."

Luke 4:1-3

Did Jesus have the power to turn stone into bread? Absolutely! Would it have been the best quality bread? For certain! Was Jesus hungry enough? Definitely! His flesh must have been screaming for food.

But Jesus was able to say no to the lust of His flesh because He was filled with the Holy Spirit, and He used the truth He knew, the Word of God, as a weapon against it.

> But Jesus answered him, saying, "It is written, 'Man shall not live by bread alone, but by every word of God.'"
>
> Luke 4:4

Jesus put the Word of God—the voice of God—in a higher priority than the voice of mammon. The lust of His flesh was not louder in His heart than the Word of God.

This trick of the lust of the flesh is also mentioned in Mark 4:19: "...the desires for other things." This word for desires is the Greek word epithumia, which means "desire, passionate longing, eagerness for, inordinate desire, and lust." Anything we desire that will simply gratify our natural senses cannot be what leads us, or there will be negative consequences.

Later on, we will discuss further how to achieve freedom from and victory over these traps of the enemy, not just the lust of the flesh but every trick of the spirit of mammon! But for now, I want to continue to look at other forms the lust of the flesh can take.

Fear of Missing Out

Fear Of Missing Out (FOMO) has become a quite common motivating factor in our culture today. We see our neighbors get the latest gadget, so we think we need it, too. A friend goes on a vacation abroad and we feel disappointed we don't have those same resources. We see a happy couple and wish we had that kind of relationship with our spouses.

Especially with the expansion of social media, we compare the current status of our everyday lives to the highlights of the lives of others. Things that are, in fact, unique and uncommon change our concept of what is "normal," and we feel like we are worse off than those around us.

The concept of the fear of missing out can be summarized by one very recognizable word: covetousness. Regardless of whether the cause comes from what we see on social media, among our friends, around coworkers, or just those in our neighborhoods, it is essentially the same voice. The spirit of mammon is trying to lure us into covetousness via the idea that we are missing out, that somehow God is holding out on us or favoring someone else.

The First Case of FOMO

The very first example of FOMO can be found in Genesis, when the serpent tempted Eve:

> *And out of the ground the Lord God made every tree grow that is pleasant to the sight and good for food. The tree of life was also in the midst of the garden, and the tree of the knowledge of good and evil.*
>
> Genesis 2:9

Adam and Eve had access to *every single tree* in the garden of Eden. Although it seems they weren't even tempted by it, they could have even eaten from the tree of life! God had literally given them *everything*. He was *not* holding out on them. Yet, somehow, the devil convinced Eve that He was.

Now the serpent was more cunning than any beast of the field which the Lord God had made. And he said to the woman, "Has God indeed said, 'You shall not eat of every tree of the garden?" And the woman said to the serpent, "We may eat the fruit of the trees of the garden; but of the fruit of the tree which is in the midst of the garden, God has said, 'You shall not eat it, nor shall you touch it, lest you die.'" Then the serpent said to the woman, "You will not surely die. For God knows that in the day you eat of it your eyes will be opened, and you will be like God, knowing good and evil."

Genesis 3:1-5

There is so much here in this scripture passage we could unpack, but I want to focus on this lie that God was somehow withholding something good from Adam and Eve.

First, he manipulated Eve into focusing on the *one* tree she was not allowed to eat the fruit of. She had access to every tree in existence, yet the voice of mammon got her to highlight the one thing she was not allowed to have.

The first step in allowing the voice of mammon to draw us away from trusting in God is by ignoring all of the blessings in our lives and focusing on what we don't have.

For example, you don't have an expensive sports car? Well, what about the dependable vehicle you *do* have? You don't have a car at all? What about the public transportation opportunities around you that you can take advantage of? There aren't any buses in your area? You have a cell phone and resources to call an Uber! Maybe there is a friend who is more than willing to give you a ride when necessary. Hey, praise God for your legs that allow you to walk or ride a bicycle!

There is *always* reason to give thanks to God, but the more we focus on what we do not have, the easier it is for the voice of mammon to make us feel that God is holding out on us. Somehow, we begin to believe that the God who loves us, who created us, who wants nothing but good for us is actually out to get us!

The second part of this temptation to spark Eve's fear of missing out was when the devil said, *"...and you will be like God,"* implying that she was not already like God. However, the Bible states very clearly, *"So God created man in His own image; in the image of God He created him; male and female He created them"* (Genesis 1:27).

The *truth* was that Adam and Eve were *already* like God! Eating this fruit wouldn't make them any more like God than they already were. It was a false perception, a fear of missing out that had absolutely no basis in fact.

Allowing the spirit of mammon to bring resentment and bitterness to your heart will lead you straight into sin, just like it did Eve. She focused on the one thing God withheld from her (for her own good, I might add!), and it led to her destruction. She then let the devil deceive her into thinking that by disobeying God she could somehow improve her already perfect situation!

Allowing this to happen to your heart will actually hinder your ability to receive all the good God has in store for you. Just like Eve already had access to the tree of life—the ability to live forever in her perfect, God-like state—she lost that access by allowing herself to fall for the lies of the enemy.

If you truly believe that God is withholding good things from you, your faith will be hindered. It's like if you tried to run a race with a severe injury to your leg. You may believe you can make it to the finish line, but you feel it's impossible to win first place.

You cannot believe that God is holding out on you and still believe He will provide for your needs and bring victory in your life! God is not double-minded, so we cannot be either.

Let's go back to James:

> *But let him ask in faith, with no doubting, for he who doubts is like a wave of the sea driven and tossed by the wind. For let not that man suppose that he will receive anything from the Lord; he is a double-minded man, unstable in all his ways.*
>
> James 1:6-8

Whatever may be going wrong in your life—it is *not God's fault*. We live in a fallen world, surrounded by fallen human beings. Mankind was given free will in the beginning, and unfortunately it is sometimes used to do evil. Evil is in the fallen state of our world. Our good Father God is not responsible for the negative aspects of life. God is good! Jesus says in John 10:10:

> *The thief does not come except to steal, and to kill, and to destroy. I have come that they may have life, and that they may have it more abundantly.*

Don't allow the voice of mammon to bring unbelief into your heart. Keep your eyes focused on the goodness of God, on everything He has given you, on your true identity as a child of the Most High. Then you will be able to receive all the good He has in store for you!

Covetousness

Jesus taught a parable about covetousness when a brother came to him with a disagreement regarding the inheritance his parents had left behind.

> Then one from the crowd said to Him, "Teacher, tell my brother to divide the inheritance with me."
>
> But He said to him, "Man, who made Me a judge or an arbitrator over you?" And He said to them, "Take heed and beware of covetousness, for one's life does not consist in the abundance of the things he possesses."
>
> Then He spoke a parable to them, saying: "The ground of a certain rich man yielded plentifully. And he thought within himself, saying, 'What shall I do, since I have no room to store my crops?' So he said, 'I will do this: I will pull down my barns and build greater, and there I will store all my crops and my goods. And I will say to my soul, "Soul, you have many goods laid up for many years; take your ease; eat, drink, and be merry."' But God said to him, 'Fool! This night your soul will be required of you; then whose will those things be which you have provided?'
>
> "So is he who lays up treasure for himself, and is not rich toward God."
>
> Luke 12:13-21

First of all, the reason Jesus refused to get involved with the situation of this inheritance is because it should have been taken to a magistrate. Him making a judgment would have required Jesus to take on a civil, legal, natural-world position to which He was not called.

In fact, a common misconception of the Messiah was that He *would* overthrow the Roman government and establish a natural kingdom. However, this was not His purpose, so He instead focused on the spiritual significance of this situation presented to Him.

This man felt his brother had cheated him out of his rightful share of this inheritance. Two brothers—a bond that should be stronger than any amount of money—were being torn apart by fighting over possessions. Family feuds very often come down to a love of money! Covetousness will take you places you never wanted to go, including the destruction of relationships.

However, Jesus warns us here about covetousness. He said it's not worth it! You cannot judge the richness of your life based on the abundance, or lack, of your natural possessions. Although the Word gives us warnings about riches, none of these warnings are saying that we cannot have wealth.

Look at Abraham, Solomon, King David, the Israelites leaving Egypt—examples of wealth being a blessing go on and on throughout Scripture. It doesn't matter how much stuff we have as long as that stuff doesn't have us!

As we increase financially, it is easy to begin to put our trust and confidence in the security that wealth provides. Our trust starts to be in how big our savings account or emergency fund is, rather than in God as our Provider.

That is exactly what was happening in the parable Jesus told in Luke 12. The man had filled up his barns with the increase of his crops, but he wanted even more security. So rather than giving to God of his excess, he just built bigger barns to allow more of a cushion of resources upon which he could rely. He thought, *Hey, now I have way more than enough! I can take it easy because I will never run out.*

God called this man a fool and pointed out that: 1) his possessions can't protect him from death and; 2) he can't take any of it with him when he dies. This man put his trust in his wealth rather than in God, and it brought his downfall.

The voice of mammon, of greed, of covetousness was speaking to this man. Rather than hoarding his resources for himself, he should have been giving. He could have even taken his excess seed and invested it by sharing with other farmers. He could have struck a good deal by giving his goods away, especially if they repaid him by a percentage of their own increase.

Instead, he did something similar to the parable of the talents Jesus taught in Matthew 25. The unwise servant buried his talent, and his master called him wicked and slothful. He said, *"You ought to have deposited my money with the bankers, and at my coming I would have received back my own with interest"* (Matthew 25:27).

It's not wrong to have savings. In fact, having savings is wise! However, if you are withholding with the wrong motive, thinking you need to keep it for your own security and placing your trust in that savings, you are listening to the voice of mammon.

Lack doesn't always come because of money you *don't* have; lack can come because of money you *do* have that you *shouldn't* have.

> *There is one who scatters, yet increases more; and there is one who withholds more than is right, but it leads to poverty.*
>
> Proverbs 11:24

The spirit of mammon will convince you to keep more than you should, which will not result in wealth, but in poverty.

It is possible to withhold more than is right, just like the man in this parable did. Putting your hope and security in your possessions is a dangerous position. God may tell you to give all of it away! But if that is where you put your trust, and if you are constantly comparing yourself—your wealth and possessions—with others, it will be impossible for you to fully trust God.

That is where the man in Luke 12 got it all wrong. Now, you *can* be at ease, at peace, in a place free from worry about provision. In fact, as you read further in Luke 12, that is what Jesus goes on to emphasize: that we should not worry about our natural needs, for God knows we have them. He feeds and clothes birds and lilies, how much more will He provide for His children!

The Trap of Jealousy

I remember once when a neighbor of ours got a new truck. Man, it was a beauty! I thought to myself how much I would really like a new truck, also. Then around two weeks later, the same neighbor bought a second new truck!

It was at this point I began to gripe and complain a little bit. I was still driving around an old vehicle. Why did he need *two* new trucks?

Then the Lord used one of my own sweet children to give me a wake-up call. He said, "Dad, why do you care he has two new trucks? It's because you don't have a brand-new truck!" He was right! I was jealous, not because he had two new trucks, but because I didn't have a new truck. I felt like I was missing out due to my *lack* of having a new truck.

Most of the time, the reason we get upset about someone else's big house or nice car or yacht is because *we don't have* a similar big house, nice car, or yacht. It isn't their blessing we have a problem with, it's our perception that somehow God is holding out on *us* because we don't have the same!

When I received that correction from the Lord, via my own child, I changed my attitude very quickly! And it's a good thing I did, because very soon after that I was given a brand-new truck. In fact, *my* new truck was better than my neighbor's new trucks!

The prosperity of another person has nothing to do with you—it's between that person and God! We need to stop getting offended by the prosperity of other people. If your friend is given a car, don't think, *Man, I wish I had a rich friend to give me a car!* Instead, think, *Praise God, I want to be the rich friend to give someone else a car!*

Remember, the reason the grass is greener on the other side of the fence might be because that is where the septic tank is! Just because you see someone who is financially wealthy, you don't necessarily know what is going on underneath. If we allow ourselves to become bitter over the success of others, it will be very difficult for us to receive our own blessings from God.

Covetousness does not lead to a good place.

The Destination of Covetousness

We can actually see where covetousness leads by looking into the past. Judas' story shows a clear regression as he walked down the path of covetousness. Unfortunately, as with anyone caught in this trap of mammon, it did not end well for him.

One night, Jesus and His disciples were eating a meal at the home of Lazarus, whom Jesus had raised from the dead.

> *Then Mary took a pound of very costly oil of spike-nard, anointed the feet of Jesus, and wiped His feet with her hair. And the house was filled with the fragrance of the oil. But one of His disciples, Judas Iscariot, Simon's son, who would betray Him, said, "Why was this fragrant oil not sold for three hundred denarii and given to the poor?"*
>
> John 12:3-5

Have you heard similar things said of wealthy people? I can think of a really clear example of Christians speaking this way about other Christians. A very prominent friend of mine travels the world to minister the Gospel. One thing that enables him to minister so widely is the fact that he owns a private jet.

Oh, man, do the covetous Christians come out in droves over this! "He could sell that jet and feed thousands of hungry people!" They are so offended by his prosperity!

It certainly sounds holy, doesn't it? Don't waste, give to the poor! This may come as a shock, but when you hear criticism of someone's blessing, disguised as piousness, it is not coming from a place of love. It isn't from a pure heart. It is ugly covetousness, jealousy, and greed disguised as holiness.

In fact, the Bible exposed Judas' heart:

> *This he said, not that he cared for the poor, but because he was a thief, and had the money box; and he used to take what was put in it.*
>
> John 12:6

The audacity! Judas didn't want the money for the poor, he wanted it for himself. And that is the truth of the matter. The majority of people who are bitter about the blessing of someone else wouldn't use that money to bless others—they would use it upon their own lusts of the flesh, just like Judas did.

So, Judas was simply jealous that Mary chose to use her wealth to bless Jesus. He wished he had that bottle of spikenard to sell and keep the money for himself. Jesus was being worshipped and he was not.

The devil himself is intimately acquainted with how covetousness can result in a person's downfall. As an angel, he wanted to be like God, to have all of the worship for himself. His pride and jealousy were his undoing. Now he uses this trick to bring about our own destruction as well, just like he did with Judas.

Right after this situation with the spikenard being used to anoint Jesus, Judas was so offended he went to the chief priests to offer to betray Jesus to them.

> Then one of the twelve, called Judas Iscariot, went to the chief priests and said, "What are you willing to give me if I deliver Him to you?" And they counted out to him thirty pieces of silver. So from that time he sought opportunity to betray Him.
>
> Matthew 26:14-16

Why would Judas take such drastic action simply because of jealousy and greed? Let's look back at 1 Timothy:

> For the love of money is the root of all evil. While coveting after money, some have strayed from the

faith and pierced themselves through with many sorrows.

1 Timothy 6:10 Modern English Version

Judas had a love-of-money problem and it led to evil in his life. And just like the scripture says, it also resulted in him being pierced through with many sorrows to the point where he committed suicide.

Covetousness—the lust of the flesh, the voice of the spirit of mammon—will turn you away from the Lord. This road is one you want to avoid at all costs! Notice that it begins subtly, with holy-sounding logic that criticizes the blessing of the Lord on the life of another believer. In Judas' case, it ended in deep regret and ultimately his death.

The consequences may not be this severe in your own life. However, at the very least, it will hinder your ability to freely receive every good thing God has for you! Don't fall for the temptation of sensual gratification. Keep your eyes on Jesus, trust in Him, allow Him to fulfill every need, and follow His voice alone.

3

THE LUST OF THE EYES

Many of us instinctively think that the lust of the eyes must refer to something sexual. However, this particular device of the spirit of mammon has nothing at all to do with seeing that type of gratification. The lust of the eyes has everything to do with greed!

Let's look at how it is defined in the Amplified Bible, Classic Edition:

> ...the lust of the eyes [greedy longings of the mind]....
> 1 John 2:16

Wealth and riches are often joined with power. After all, when you are wealthy, many doors of influence are opened to you as a result. So, when people see opportunity for financial increase, or promotion that comes with power, influence, and authority, this is the perfect time for the spirit of mammon to start talking!

What it comes down to is one simple word: greed. Whether it is for money, position, power, or prestige, it all comes from empty promises. Money will make you happy. Power will give you the opportunity to make change. Prestige, or popularity, will ensure that other people treat you well, or even fairly at the very least.

Yet all these things are lies. They are a façade, giving only a surface image of success. Externally, you may experience benefits of wealth, power, prestige, or notoriety, but none of these things will bring lasting satisfaction.

Greedy Longings

We can see Eve fall into this trap right after she saw that it was going to be a yummy treat:

> So when the woman saw...that it was pleasant to the eyes....
>
> Genesis 3:6

As mentioned briefly previously, the Hebrew word here for *pleasant* is *taavah,* which means "dainty, desire, exceedingly, greedily, lusting, pleasant." It doesn't just mean it looked nice, although that was probably true.

In Numbers 11:4, the New American Standard Bible, this same word is translated, *"...had greedy cravings."* The sight of this fruit sparked a greedy craving inside of Eve and she just had to have it!

Unfortunately, the greedy longings of her mind, resulted in her being drawn into disobedience by the spirit of mammon. How sad, when—as I pointed out in the last chapter—Eve had complete access to all other delicious trees in the Garden! There was absolutely no reason for her to desire this fruit.

In a similar way, the devil tried to tempt Jesus through the lie of greed.

> Then the devil, taking Him up on a high mountain, showed Him all the kingdoms of the world in a moment of time. And the devil said to Him, "All this authority I will give You, and their glory; for this has

*been delivered to me, and I give it to whomever I
wish. Therefore, if You will worship before me, all will
be Yours."*

Luke 4:5-7

The devil used a very similar strategy when he tempted
Jesus as he did when he tempted Eve. He tried to tempt Jesus
with something that already belonged to Him. Yes, the earth
was under the enemy's authority at that time, so that was a
partial truth. When God created humanity, He gave Adam
and Eve dominion over the entire earth. However, when they
sinned, they gave that authority to the devil.

For more information on this subject, get our booklet enti-
tled *Your Life with God.* It goes into more detail regarding the
fall of man, the consequences of the fall, as well as how God
used Jesus to get it back!

Yet, Jesus is God! He already had all authority, all glory,
and the earth already belonged to Him (Psalm 24:1). The devil
was tempting Jesus with power and authority He already had.

Jealousy, greed, and lust for power were the temptations
that caused the devil to be cast out of heaven in the first place.
He had wanted the universe to worship him rather than God
(Isaiah 14:12-14), and those desires never left him. If he could
get Jesus, the divine Son of God, the Messiah to worship him,
then it would all be over! The world would be completely in
his hands!

In fact, if Jesus had submitted to any of the three temptations He faced here in the wilderness, it would have been a
sign that He was worshipping the devil as god, giving satan
the ultimate authority over both Him and the rest of the world.

However, Jesus didn't fall for the voice of mammon.

You know, Hebrews 4:15 tells us that Jesus was tempted in every way we are, yet He was without sin. Yet again, Jesus fought the deception of the enemy with the Word of God.

And Jesus answered and said to him, "Get behind Me, Satan! For it is written, 'You shall worship the Lord your God, and Him only you shall serve.'"

Luke 4:8

Remember this lesson: sometimes when the voice of mammon comes whispering in your ear, you just have to say, "Get behind me, devil!" He is all talk. All bark, and no bite!

Be sober, be vigilant; because your adversary the devil walks about like a roaring lion, seeking whom he may devour.

1 Peter 5:8

Notice that this verse says the devil walks around like a roaring lion. He is not a lion! He is a liar, who yells really loudly, insisting upon your fear and attention in response. He is simply masquerading as a lion, dressed up in all the gear, yet the claws and teeth are made of rubber. He is nothing for us to fear.

When they were young, we used to play a little game with our children called, "Real or Fake?" We would ask about television characters like, "Is Barney real or fake?" or natural subjects like, "Is the wind real or fake?" And other times we would want them to really give the question some serious thought, like, "Are nightmares real or fake?"

One day we posed the question, "Is the devil real or fake?" and our daughter, Hannah, gave us a very insightful answer!

She thought for a moment before responding, "Both! The devil is real, but his weapons are fake."

Wow! The wisdom that comes from simple, childlike faith can blow your mind sometimes, because she was right on target! The devil is real, yes. He is a spiritual being who dwells in the spiritual realm, yet he can influence the natural realm. However, all of his weapons are fake; they are lies meant to draw our attention away from the truth of the Word of God!

If the devil can distract us into believing his lies, or submitting to his fake weapons and powerless roar, he can render our power ineffective. First Peter 5:8 says he is seeking those whom he may devour. This implies that in order for him to actually devour us, we must give our consent and allow him access. Otherwise, he may not devour us!

No matter what he says or how loudly he roars, if you use the Word of God—spoken from your own mouth with faith—you can shut him up.

Seeing Beyond the Natural

In Mark 4, Jesus correlated this lust of the eyes—greedy longings of the mind—with the deceitfulness of riches. This trap is a thorn that can crush the life out of the seed of the Word that you have planted in your heart. This is probably the most pervasive of the enemy's traps when it comes to keeping believers from living in the abundance Jesus died for us to have.

As I mentioned earlier, we live in a physical world, and everything in it will try to get us to trust in the way it functions in the natural. As a result, our minds are literally wired to see every aspect of life through this lens. It affects our behaviors, yes, but more importantly, it affects what we believe is possible.

We have all grown up being taught the natural way the world functions. When we get sick, we go to the doctor. In a financial crisis, we get a second or third job. If we want a *good* job, we need to go to college. To prepare for a big expense, we should save enough, or we won't be able to afford it. We need to build up our credit score to buy a house and get a good interest rate.

If the housing market in a certain area is such that it has caused prices to skyrocket, you won't get a good deal, so don't even try. If you don't have that college degree, just try to settle for a career that is more realistic than the one you want. If you were born with a genetic condition, well, that's just the way it is.

Some of these statements may appear factual in the natural, however, the Word of God gives promises that trump all of them! It says by the stripes of Jesus, we were healed (1 Peter 2:24). That Jesus became poor so that we could be rich (2 Corinthians 8:9). The Bible tells us that we have the mind of Christ, and God's favor surrounds us with a shield! (1 Corinthians 2:16 and Psalm 5:12.)

I could go on and on, but my point is this: every negative situation we may face in this natural world, God has given us a supernatural solution. If our minds are trained to only see natural solutions to natural problems, the enemy can easily mislead us with the voice of mammon! We will look to natural actions to help solve natural problems, and this is how the Word becomes choked with the deceitfulness of riches.

Remember, we can't serve two masters. Mammon wants us to serve him, not God. However, our relationship with God is not purely one of servant and master—it is the close relationship of a Father and child.

Mammon will try to get in the way of our relationship with God. It will say, "You need to trust in money. You need x amount of dollars in the bank before you can be secure. You need a job that pays x amount per hour or per year before you can rest." But the promises God has given us in His Word say something entirely different.

The Rich Young Ruler

There's a story of a young man who came to Jesus for advice:

> Now as He was going out on the road, one came running, knelt before Him, and asked Him, "Good Teacher, what shall I do that I may inherit eternal life?"
>
> So Jesus said to him, "Why do you call Me good? No one is good but One, that is, God. You know the commandments: 'Do not commit adultery,' 'Do not murder,' 'Do not steal,' 'Do not bear false witness,' 'Do not defraud,' 'Honor your father and your mother.'"
>
> And he answered and said to Him, "Teacher, all these things I have kept from my youth."
>
> Then Jesus, looking at him, loved him, and said to him, "One thing you lack: Go your way, sell whatever you have and give to the poor, and you will have treasure in heaven; and come, take up the cross, and follow Me."
>
> But he was sad at this word, and went away sorrowful, for he had great possessions.
>
> Mark 10:17-22

This young man came to Jesus to ask an important question about eternity. I believe that Jesus' response was His attempt to prompt this rich young ruler to see how much he needed a Savior. The law is impossible to follow perfectly. No human being is able to live a perfectly sinless life (Romans 3:23); that's why blood sacrifices were established under the Old Covenant and why Jesus had to shed His own blood under the New.

Unfortunately, this young man was already deceived, because he felt he had followed the law perfectly. So, again, trying to show this man that he *needed* help—a Savior—to attain eternal life, Jesus spoke directly to the voice of mammon that had been speaking to him.

Jesus knew by the Holy Spirit—He received a word of wisdom—that this young man was trusting in mammon more than in God. He knew this guy had been trusting in riches; and unless he rejected his trust in his wealth, and put his trust in God instead, the deceitfulness of riches would still have him trapped.

Some of these things I am saying might seem just as harsh as Jesus telling this young man to sell all of his possessions. But Jesus looked at the rich young ruler and *loved him.* Jesus loves you, too! He doesn't want the devil getting your attention, your service, your loyalty. He wants your ear 100 percent because He has such good things for you!

Some people use this scripture passage in Mark 10 to justify their belief that God wants us to be poor, completely destitute. They also can go to the extreme believing that no one who is wealthy can enter eternity with God!

However, they aren't looking at the context closely at all! By telling this man, *"One thing you lack...sell whatever you have...and follow Me,"* Jesus was attempting a second time to show the rich young man how much he was trusting in and listening to the wrong voice. His trust was entirely in his own ability to follow the law and his wealth—not at all in God!

This fellow was rich, young, and a ruler; he had everything going for him! But Jesus told him he only needed to do one thing—stop trusting in his riches and trust in God.

But the rich young ruler missed it. He went away sad at Jesus' word because he was truly wealthy. His financial house was in order and all his bills were more than paid. If he wasn't already married, he would have had his choice of beautiful women to marry. He had it all! Except, he didn't have a relationship with God, and that is the one thing Jesus said we all need to have eternal life (John 17:3).

The young man was trying to serve two masters, God and mammon, but that's just not possible. God said, "Give it all away and trust Me," but mammon's voice said, "You can't do that! You have to trust me! Without me, you won't have any security!" He walked away from Jesus very sorrowful because mammon's voice was stronger in his life than Jesus' voice.

Anytime we've missed it, we can look back and usually see we were following the deceptive voice of mammon—the logic of this natural world—rather than following the voice of God. If we are saddened or offended by a word from God, it reveals to us our hearts have put more trust in mammon than in the Lord.

After the young man left, Jesus addressed His disciples:

> Then Jesus looked around and said to His disciples, "How hard it is for those who have riches to enter the kingdom of God!" And the disciples were astonished at His words. But Jesus answered again and said to them, "Children, how hard it is for those who trust in riches to enter the kingdom of God! It is

easier for a camel to go through the eye of a needle than for a rich man to enter the kingdom of God."

And they were greatly astonished, saying among themselves, "Who then can be saved?"

But Jesus looked at them and said, "With men it is impossible, but not with God; for with God all things are possible."

Mark 10:23-27

Why were the disciples so surprised when Jesus told them how difficult it was for the wealthy to enter the Kingdom of God? Well, these guys weren't really poor! Most of them were business owners, fishermen and tax collectors!

They were probably thinking, *But we've got money! Are we stuck?* But Jesus clarified in verse 24 that the problem is for those who *trust* in riches. It's not about *having* riches. For those who do have wealth, it is more challenging to see God as their source and security. The problem comes when we trust in riches over trusting in God.

If we trust in mammon, it will pull us away from listening to the voice of God clearly and doing what God wants us to do. Yet, this is really hard sometimes because we can feel if we fully obey when He tells us to give, there could be very scary consequences!

However, we need to look at how Jesus summed up what seemed to be a very difficult request:

Then Peter began to say to Him, "See, we have left all and followed You."

So Jesus answered and said, "Assuredly, I say to you, there is no one who has left house or brothers or sisters or father or mother or wife or children or lands, for My sake and the gospel's, who shall not receive a hundredfold now in this time—houses and brothers and sisters and mothers and children and lands, with persecutions—and in the age to come, eternal life."

Mark 10:28-30

Here Jesus was giving them comfort and assurance because He knows how difficult it is for us to disregard the security that comes from wealth and put our trust 100 percent in God. He isn't insensitive to this struggle!

However, He promises us that if we put our trust in Him and follow His direction, we won't be losing out on anything! He promises we will receive a 100-fold return without carrying the burden that comes when we trust in riches alone.

Whoever loves money never has enough; whoever loves wealth is never satisfied with their income. This too is meaningless.

Ecclesiastes 5:10 New International Version

Having riches will never be enough to satisfy us. Wealth absent a relationship with our loving Father God is meaningless. However, when our foundation is based on intimate fellowship with God, money can be an asset to the Kingdom of God. The key is keeping our trust in God rather than in mammon.

Being Content

I believe we should always be looking toward increase in our lives. However, we need to check our hearts to ensure our desire for increase is not to spend it upon our own lusts, but to be able to give more and more to others.

One of the biggest problems believers have with this is that it seems greedy. And I understand that. However, throughout Scripture wealth is spoken of as a blessing, and poverty is described as a curse. This is one way we know God's perspective of wealth and finances. He sees wealth as a blessing and poverty as a curse. If He didn't, He wouldn't have written it that way! However, we can still learn to be content regardless of present circumstances.

Not that I speak in regard to need, for I have learned in whatever state I am, to be content.

Philippians 4:11

Paul learned to be content, no matter what his situation was. Whether he was wealthy or struggling, full or hungry, he was content. So how can we be content yet still believe for and expect increase?

Mammon will tell you it is holy to be poor, but that is a lie. However, mammon will also tell you that being content is passive. That is also a lie! The word *content* actually indicates living in a state of faith in God—it is the Greek word *autarkés*, which actually means "sufficiency within." Contentment is an inward adequacy that comes through the indwelling power of Jesus. It is literally suggesting an ability that comes from Jesus.

Being content in whatever state you are doesn't mean you don't believe your state can improve, increase, or get better! It means you are standing in faith that no matter the circumstances in which you find yourself, you know Jesus has given you the power to overcome. That is why Paul ended with this statement:

> I can do all things through Christ who strengthens me.
>
> Philippians 4:13

This scripture is found in the middle of Paul talking about finances. Handling your finances by listening to God's voice, avoiding covetousness, and staying content—it is all accomplished by the grace of God, the power of Jesus in you.

Where is your motivation for increase? Do you want more because it will bring you more material comfort? Will having more make you feel like a success; will you find your identity in wealth? Or do you want more so you can give toward the Kingdom? If your heart is Kingdom and God-minded, don't ever feel condemned for believing for increase. God wants to bring increase to those who will use it well.

The first time I got a Cadillac, I was excited, but not for the reason you might expect. The minute I sat in the driver's seat and placed my hands on the wheel, I knew that car wasn't mine. I was meant to give it away!

The Lord told me, "This isn't your car." I was so excited, wondering who I would give it to.

Ultimately, I gave it to a couple whose car had just basically blown up. So, we had this extra Cadillac Carlie had been driving and I told them, "You can borrow Carlie's car," knowing I was going to give it to them.

When I brought it to work to give it to them, I gave them the keys, but when they saw it, they said, "We can't borrow this car, it's just too nice! We are too nervous to drive around a car this nice." They had always driven older, broken-down cars and just had this idea they weren't worthy of driving something so nice.

I said, "Well, that works out, then, because I'm not lending it to you, I'm giving it to you." So I signed over the title to them right there!

This turned out to be huge for them because it broke that poverty mentality they had had, specifically regarding the vehicles they drove. In fact, I had programmed a message on the dash panel that said, "You are blessed," every time they turned it on!

A week later, someone else gave them a nice car as well, and from that point on, they never drove another junker car ever again!

Giving in Faith

Our daughter was dying, and doctors had given her a week to live. That very week, Andrew Wommack Ministries happened to be holding a conference in England, and we took our daughter there for prayer for her healing.

The first night, they took up an offering. I wanted to give to Andrew's ministry because he was the one who taught us for the first time that it is *always* God's will to heal. Knowing that truth is what gave us the confidence to ask God in faith to heal Hannah.

I prayed and asked God how much to give, and God told me, *"Give everything you've got, right now."* Now, that'll get your attention! At first I was plugging my ears and singing, "I can't hear You, Lord!"

As I had that initial reaction, it dawned on me that my trust was in money, not in God, and I hadn't even realized it! If you had asked me if I trusted 100 percent in God, I would have said yes. But I would have been wrong. That initial fear response was the catalyst I needed to see that my trust was misplaced.

God was challenging me, just like the rich young ruler. He was saying, "Ashley, do you trust Me?" In order for my answer to be yes, I had to trust God not only with my daughter's life, but with my finances as well. I had to be all in!

The reason I don't tell this story often when sharing the testimony of Hannah's healing is because of a misunderstanding that can very easily happen. So please hear me now: I was not buying my daughter's healing! I was not bribing God to receive a healing for my child. This had nothing at all to do with the amount of money I was giving to Andrew's ministry.

This wasn't a money issue; it was a heart issue. My heart was trusting in money—listening to the voice of mammon rather than the voice of God. So, God came along to tempt me with good, and it was my choice!

God tempted the rich young ruler with good, and it was his choice to deny it. He was saying, "Look, if you want to follow Me, I can fix this mammon problem! But in order for that to happen, you're going to have to trust Me." But the voice of mammon was too strong for him, and the young man followed after his riches rather than Jesus.

Before giving what God had led me to give, I asked Carlie. She said, "Do what He says," and we gave everything that was in our bank account. I was shaking as I wrote the check, but I put it in the offering. Something in my heart shifted, and I decided to put my trust in God, rather than in mammon. Natural resources, my money, no longer had a hold on my heart!

The next day, my daughter received her healing, not because I gave some amount of money, but because something had changed in my heart. Since then, we've never looked back; financially we have prospered because I learned to trust in God, not in mammon.

This is so much more than money. The voice of mammon, trying to get you to trust in the natural world, will stop you from receiving from God in *all* ways. It will choke the Word and make it unfruitful. If you are looking at your life and wondering why the Word isn't working, it's not the Word that's the problem, but the deceitfulness of riches, the worries that come from looking only at the natural realm. The spirit of mammon has a chokehold on you, and it is keeping the Word from bearing fruit in your life.

The Prodigal Son

The story of the Prodigal Son is another valuable lesson regarding the price we pay when we allow the deceitfulness of riches to distract us.

> Then He said: "A certain man had two sons. And the younger of them said to his father, 'Father, give me the portion of goods that falls to me.' So he divided to them his livelihood."
>
> Luke 15:11-12

This young man had a good family, a good job helping run the family business, and a good future filled with success ahead of him. However, he asked his dad if he could cash in on his share of their property early so he could have some fun!

Here, the voice of mammon was speaking loudly using the deceitfulness of riches. Although this guy apparently had a good life, he saw a better life if he had more money to spend. Let's see how that worked out:

And not many days after, the younger son gathered all together, journeyed to a far country, and there wasted his possessions with prodigal living. But when he had spent all, there arose a severe famine in that land, and he began to be in want. Then he went and joined himself to a citizen of that country, and he sent him into his fields to feed swine. And he would gladly have filled his stomach with the pods that the swine ate, and no one gave him anything.

Luke 15:13-16

This kid went to party! In verse 13, the word *prodigal* is *asótós*, which means "extravagantly wasteful." This young man will be known forever as "the wasteful son"! He thought his life would be better off with all of that money, but it was a lie—a deception of the voice of mammon that wanted to destroy him.

This is the same lie we fall for all the time today. We choose careers based on what we feel will make us the most money. We decide where to live based on the cost of living. We choose a college based on either what we can afford or if we feel it will result in a higher income later on.

These things are so untrustworthy! God has our best interests at heart, and if we aren't listening to His voice, we will end up making the wrong choices, which can result in our lives going in negative directions.

Thankfully, this isn't the end of the story, not for the Prodigal Son, and not for those of us who have made similar mistakes and fallen victim to the voice of mammon.

But when he came to himself, he said, "How many of my father's hired servants have bread enough and to spare, and I perish with hunger! I will arise and go to my father, and will say to him, 'Father, I have sinned against heaven and before you, and I am no longer worthy to be called your son. Make me like one of your hired servants.'" And he arose and came to his father. But when he was still a great way off, his father saw him and had compassion, and ran and fell on his neck and kissed him. And the son said to him, "Father, I have sinned against heaven and in your sight, and am no longer worthy to be called your son." But the father said to his servants, "Bring out the best robe and put it on him, and put a ring on his hand and sandals on his feet. And bring the fatted calf here and kill it, and let us eat and be merry; for this my son was dead and is alive again; he was lost and is found." And they began to be merry.

Luke 15:17-24

The young man realized he had left his father, who would have supplied everything he needed, and more! And when he returned, his father received him with open arms, complete forgiveness, and unconditional love and favor!

If you can see how you have been drawn away by mammon's lying voice, just come back to the Father! He is ready to receive you in the same way.

The unfortunate part of this story is how this young man's brother reacted to the situation. He responded with covetousness.

Now his older son was in the field. And as he came and drew near to the house, he heard music and dancing. So he called one of the servants and asked what these things meant. And he said to him, "Your brother has come, and because he has received him safe and sound, your father has killed the fatted calf." But he was angry and would not go in. Therefore his father came out and pleaded with him. So he answered and said to his father, "Lo, these many years I have been serving you; I never transgressed your commandment at any time; and yet you never gave me a young goat, that I might make merry with my friends. But as soon as this son of yours came, who has devoured your livelihood with harlots, you killed the fatted calf for him." And he said to him, "Son, you are always with me, and all that I have is yours."

Luke 15:25-31

The brother had absolutely nothing to be jealous of. His father said, "All I have is yours!" He already owned everything his father owned. He could have taken a goat or a calf to party with his friends at any time. It was all already his for the taking, but he never received what already belonged to him.

This is what happens to us so many times. We see our brother or sister in Christ receive a blessing or favor from God, and we think to ourselves, *That's not fair! What about me, God?* In reality, it all belongs to us! Perhaps it is the attitude of our hearts, of covetousness and jealousy, that is keeping us from freely receiving what the Father has already freely given.

For example, let's say, when they were young, I took one of my sons shopping for his birthday. We go out and I buy him everything he could possibly want: a new bike, a gaming system, a bunch of clothes. When we come home, how would my other son react?

Would he be jealous? Would he think, *That's not fair! How come he gets all of this? What about me?* No, that's not the reaction he would have. Rather than being covetous, he would be happy for his brother!

He would think, *That's awesome! If Dad bought* him *all of that stuff, soon it's going to be my turn! Dad is going to be just as generous with me!*

In the same way, we should rejoice with just as much excitement when our brothers and sisters in Christ succeed and are blessed. If my Father God did it for them, He will certainly do it for me! He doesn't play favorites, and His blessing and promises are for me as much as any other believer.

Our Father God has already provided for us blessing, favor, increase, and success. There is no place in our hearts for covetousness because all He has is already ours. Receive it by faith today and stay in a place of thankfulness. Then hang on because you will begin to see what you have believed!

4

THE PRIDE OF LIFE

Now we've come to the most common tactic of the voice of mammon. These whispers come every single day, in nearly every decision we make. Interestingly, this trap doesn't directly apply to money.

> *...and the pride of life [assurance in one's own resources or in the stability of earthly things]—these do not come from the Father but are from the world [itself].*
>
> 1 John 2:16 AMPC

This temptation to fall into mammon's trap usually presents itself in a subtly prideful way. Remember how when Judas was tempted through covetousness, he used a false caring for the poor to disguise his greed? In a similar way, the enemy uses strategies disguised as humility when they are truthfully rooted in pride.

The word translated *pride* in 1 John 2:16 is the Greek word *alazoneia*, which means "boastfulness" and "arrogant display."

The word *life* is the Greek word *bios* which refers to biological life, but also has other connotations. One is the manner in which you live your life, and the other refers to one's livelihood.

In fact, this word *bios* is the same word found in Luke 15:12 in the story of the Prodigal Son.

And the younger of them said to his father, "Father give me the portion of goods that falls to me." So he divided to them his livelihood.

We see this sort of arrogant confidence in one's own resources whenever someone boasts about their profession: doctor, lawyer, engineer, politician, etc. Is it *wrong* to have any of those careers? Of course not! However, placing our confidence in the type of livelihood we make, rather than in God, will result in us following the wrong voice.

"Assurance in one's own resources" directly refers to pride. It is simply doing things your own way, thinking you can handle something on your own. Everything that needs done, you are responsible for taking care of it. Whether that takes the form of your finances, your intellect, or your own ability, the focus for provision is on yourself.

The other part of this is relying on the "stability of earthly things." This is what happened to the rich young ruler. He trusted more in his earthly wealth than in God. However, our possessions are not reliable. When we trust in things that are of the natural realm or economy, it is like we are building a house without a solid foundation.

While we do not look at the things which are seen, but at the things which are not seen. For the things which are seen are temporary, but the things which are not seen are eternal.

2 Corinthians 4:18

Natural disasters can damage physical possessions (although, when we trust in God, He can provide protection from those things). The stock market can crash (although,

God's blessing and favor can also help us increase in the midst of a downturn)!

When I was in Bible school in England, I looked into different ways of making extra money, and I decided to invest in the foreign currency exchange (Forex). I was buying and selling and made and lost money at different points throughout the years.

One day I woke up in the morning and was horrified to see that the market had completely tanked overnight! I put my head in my hands and groaned.

My son asked me, "Dad, is that a good groan or a bad groan?"

I said, "It's a bad groan."

"What should we do?" he asked me.

"Son, tell Mum to pray!" I had lost so much money. It wasn't just a small loss—it was devastating! Although it was initially a solid blow, we hadn't built our house on sand. God was our Provider, and our security wasn't in a natural thing like the Forex market. He is faithful!

Ultimately, when I closed out the accounts—due to the fluctuations in the market over those two years and converting to a new currency—I ended up coming out with a small *increase*! I didn't lose a penny, and I believe that was supernatural. We kept our eyes on God rather than on the temporary, unreliable, natural things of the world, and God revealed His faithfulness to us.

Natural resources are simply untrustworthy. They will always let us down. How do I know this?

Well, the Bible reinforces this point multiple times throughout scripture:

*...and he who earns wages, earns wages to put into
a bag with holes.*

Haggai 1:6

Have you ever felt like no matter how much your paycheck is, it's never enough? There's just always more month
at the end of the money? When we live by faith in our natural
resources alone—including our paychecks—this is exactly what
happens! Yet, God can miraculously multiply our resources
when we place our trust in Him, alone.

*Will you set your eyes on that which is not? For riches
certainly make themselves wings; they fly away like
an eagle toward heaven.*

Proverbs 23:5

Have you noticed when you are doing well financially,
you aren't as intentional about how you spend your money?
Then suddenly you realize, "Wait a minute! I was doing well!
Where'd all that money go?" Remember 2 Corinthians 4:18:
things which are *seen* are temporary. Riches are only temporary. They are unreliable and untrustworthy; there one moment
and gone the next!

*Do not put your trust in princes, nor in a son of man,
in whom there is no help. His spirit departs, he
returns to his earth; in that very day his plans perish.*

Psalm 146:3-4

We can't put our trust in other people either, even those
who are wealthy. I've seen some people say, "I believe God put
so-in-so in my path because they are very wealthy. I know they
are going to pay for what I need!" This is a very dangerous—
and unfair—attitude to have. If God speaks to that person to

be a blessing to you financially, that's fantastic! However, you cannot expect someone else to meet your needs.

You have put yourself in a position to become bitter and resentful toward someone because you placed your trust in that person rather than in God! But people are just as temporary as natural resources. You cannot trust in them any more than you can in your paycheck. Just as your wages can be placed into a bag with holes, and riches can fly off like eagles, humans are unreliable, also.

My point is: our trust must be in God. Physical things are temporary, but God is eternal and unfailing! The things of earth will let us down, but God will always be on our side.

Good to Make Wise

The third thing Eve noticed about the fruit of the tree of the knowledge of good and evil was that she saw it as a source of wisdom and success.

> So when the woman saw that the tree was good for food, that it was pleasant to the eyes, and a tree desirable to make one wise, she took of its fruit and ate. She also gave to her husband with her, and he ate.
>
> Genesis 3:6

As mentioned previously, the phrase "to make one wise" is the Hebrew word *sakal,* which means to be prudent. In other passages of scripture, it is translated to behaving wisely, having success, prospering, gaining insight or understanding." Basically, this type of wisdom or prudence would bring prosperity and success.

Apparently, Eve didn't think God was a sufficient enough source for wisdom and success! So, she took it upon herself to not only eat for herself, but give to her husband as well. As she looked for success outside of the perfect plan God had created for her, she brought about her own downfall.

> *If any of you lacks wisdom, let him ask of God, who gives to all liberally and without reproach, and it will be given to him.*
>
> James 1:5

If we need wisdom, we can ask God and He gives it liberally, generously! Our success in this life is found when we follow His voice and His leading. That type of wisdom, blessing, and increase is stable—not based on the world's system. We can rely on Him without looking to our own resources or the world to give us what we need.

Jesus' Third Temptation

The enemy tempted Jesus for a third time:

> *Then he brought Him to Jerusalem, set Him on the pinnacle of the temple, and said to Him, "If You are the Son of God, throw Yourself down from here. For it is written: 'He shall give His angels charge over you, to keep you,' and, 'In their hands they shall bear you up, lest you dash your foot against a stone.'"*
>
> *And Jesus answered and said to him, "It has been said, 'You shall not tempt the Lord your God.'"*
>
> Luke 4:9-12

Remember, I mentioned in the previous chapter that all these temptations had a similar goal: to cause Jesus to give

His authority to the devil. Here that is obvious as he presented this temptation at a place of great significance—the pinnacle of the temple, which was a place of worship, authority, and instruction.

The pinnacle of the temple stood roughly fifteen stories tall, and it was in an area of high traffic. It stood above a plaza that bordered the main road through Jerusalem. Therefore, it was a daily gathering place for hundreds, even thousands, of Jews.

Here the Jews were called to pray and remember all of the miraculous works God had done to save them. If Jesus had jumped from that height, in that public of a location, He certainly would have become famous. If angels *had* actually saved Him from death, it would have been a sure-fire way to prove to the masses that He was the Messiah!

On the other hand, if He had jumped and died before His appointed time, He would also have become famous, just in a different, more tragic way!

Satan was telling Jesus, "I know Your Father has told You His plan to reveal You as Messiah to the people, but wouldn't this be better? It would be way more efficient! You might even have a good time, too. Flying is fun!"

For Jesus to give in to this temptation, He would be turning from God's plan for His life and taking matters into His own hands. He would be relying on His own ability to strategize and take action to fulfill His calling, rather than following the leading of the Holy Spirit.

Any time we deviate from the direction God has given us to follow the voice of mammon, or to do things our own way, we are displaying "assurance in one's own resources." This is a prime example of the pride of life.

But Jesus pushed back again with the Word of God.

And Jesus answered and said to him, "It has been said, 'You shall not tempt the Lord your God.'"

Luke 4:12

Satan had quoted Psalm 91:11-12 to Jesus to justify Him throwing Himself off the temple. "Hey, don't worry about it, Jesus, the angels will catch You!" Yet, Jesus knew the heart of that scripture wasn't giving God's children permission to be foolish!

You know the saying, "Play stupid games, win stupid prizes"? That's actually pretty biblical, in my opinion! If you go jumping off a mountain on *purpose*—especially if God hasn't *told* you to jump off a mountain—you can't expect angels to catch you. Gravity is going to work, and you're going to hit the ground hard.

A prudent person foresees danger and takes precautions. The simpleton goes blindly on and suffers the consequences.

Proverbs 27:12 NLT

However, if you are hiking up a mountain and you *accidentally fall,* you can trust that God will have His angels ready and waiting to keep you from even stubbing your toe!

Sometimes this temptation, like the others, can take the form of something good. You might think, "I'm going to do this potentially risky thing to *prove* the goodness of God to people!" That seems like a good motivation; however, that's exactly what the devil was tempting Jesus to do, and Jesus said, "Nope! Don't try to test God by doing something He didn't say to do!"

The word translated *tempt* in Luke 4:12 is the Greek word *ekpeirazó*, which means "to test thoroughly, tempt" in a way that exceeds reasonable and appropriate boundaries or limits. This temptation to throw Himself off of a rooftop, expecting God to prove His Word true by sending angels to catch Him, was going too far!

> *The way of a fool is right in his own eyes, but he who heeds counsel is wise.*
>
> Proverbs 12:15

However, if God has instructed you to do something that violates natural laws, you can have faith in that situation that His power can supersede the natural. As He did with Peter, if He tells you, "Come," you can trust He will enable you to walk on water! (Matthew 14:29.)

The natural laws involved aren't the point. The important thing is to keep your ears open to the direction of the Holy Spirit—to follow God's plans for your life—rather than listening to the world, to the voice of mammon.

Did God Really Say?

The devil is a liar. In fact, Jesus said this of him: *"...He was a murderer from the beginning. He has always hated the truth, because there is no truth in him. When he lies, it is consistent with his character, for he is a liar and the father of lies"* (John 8:44 NLT).

Even when the devil quotes scripture, he will twist it, misquote it, or take it out of context to mislead us.

A great example of this is how the world has somehow adopted the saying, "Money is the root of all evil," and think it comes from the Bible. Yet, the verse actually says, *"For the* love of money *is a root of all kinds of evil, for which some have strayed from the faith in their greediness, and pierced themselves through with many sorrows"* (1 Timothy 6:10).

This deception has caused many in the church to adopt the idea that poverty is a blessing and brings glory to God. After all, if money is the root of all evil, then a good, holy, sanctified believer shouldn't pollute themselves with evil money!

Let's look at the way the devil deceived Eve by getting her to question God's Word.

> *Now the serpent was more cunning than any beast of the field which the Lord God had made. And he said to the woman, "Has God indeed said, 'You shall not eat of every tree of the garden'?"*
>
> *And the woman said to the serpent, "We may eat the fruit of the trees of the garden; but of the fruit of the tree which is in the midst of the garden, God has said, 'You shall not eat it, nor shall you touch it, lest you die.'"*
>
> Genesis 3:1-3

Notice, the devil did technically quote God's words properly. Technically, God *had* told them they couldn't eat of *every* tree in the garden. Of course, the devil omitted the part about her having access to everything else she could have possibly needed, therefore manipulating Eve into focusing on the *one thing* she wasn't supposed to have.

His main goal, however, was to get Eve to question God's Word. "Eve, did God *really* say that?" Then, the part *"nor shall you touch it,"* was an addition God hadn't said. If she thought God had said not to touch it or she would die, then touched it without the consequence of dying, it could cause her to draw the conclusion that God's Word wasn't true. It is a very dangerous thing for us to *add* to God's Word!

When the devil tempted Jesus, he did the same thing. His main attack was to question God's Word. Just prior to these temptations, in Luke 3:22, Father God had told Jesus audibly in a voice from heaven, *"You are My beloved Son, in You I am well pleased."*

So, when the father of lies came to tempt Jesus, he challenged God's Word by saying, *"If You are the Son of God...."* Satan was essentially saying, "Jesus, did God *really* say You were His Son? If so, then prove it! Cause, You don't look much like the Son of God to me."

Today, the devil will desperately try to get you to question the Word of God. Why? Because if he can get you to question what God has truly said, he can win any battle with us. Our victory comes through the Word of God, so if we don't have the utmost faith and confidence in His Word, we can be swayed to believing the lies that we are powerless and defeated.

The Ultimate Act of Pride

In this third temptation of Jesus, He was being tempted in a couple different ways.

One: to prove He was the Messiah in a way which would seemingly reach the most people.

Two: to commit suicide.

You see, pride isn't just arrogance or being boastful. At its core, pride is simply being more concerned with ourselves than anyone else, including God. Committing suicide is the most prideful, self-centered thing a human being can do.

Now, obviously people who try to kill themselves have come to a place of complete hopelessness. I am not minimizing the fact that this world is fallen, horrible things happen, and people suffer as a result. If you or a loved one have ever had these thoughts, I completely empathize. Having these thoughts is not sin! Jesus had these thoughts as well, but He didn't act on them. But my point is that those who choose to die have reached a place where they have no trust in God to help them.

One, they are looking at themselves, seeing an unlovable failure when they look in the mirror. Or they feel that life is just too difficult, too challenging.

Two, they feel God has somehow let them down. He isn't there, or He doesn't care enough to help them. The enemy has convinced them there is no hope, so the only escape they can see from their torment is death.

However, this entire temptation—every kind, really—is filled with lies!

Not all of us will face that ultimate temptation of pride: suicide. For those of us who do, it is important to understand that whatever the reasons we are considering it, they are lies. The enemy has convinced us that all hope is gone, that we are alone, that God doesn't love us or care enough about us to give us victory in our situation. *It's just not true!*

Jesus, Don't You Care?

Falling to that lowest of lows, the heart will cry out, "God, don't You care that I'm dying? Don't You love me?" Any time you begin to question God's love for you, that is a lie from the spirit of mammon!

Do you remember in Mark 4 where Jesus taught about the thorns that come in and choke the Word? On the same day He had taught them the Parable of the Sower—among many other parables—Jesus directed His disciples to go to the other side of the Sea of Galilee.

> *On the same day, when evening had come, He said to them, "Let us cross over to the other side." Now when they had left the multitude, they took Him along in the boat as He was. And other little boats were also with Him. And a great windstorm arose, and the waves beat into the boat, so that it was already filling. But He was in the stern, asleep on a pillow. And they awoke Him and said to Him, "Teacher, do You not care that we are perishing?"*
>
> Mark 4:35-38

I don't know about you, but if I were Jesus in this situation, I'd get a little annoyed! First of all, I *told* you we were going to the other side. If this storm was truly a problem, I wouldn't have said, "Let's go to the other side." I certainly wouldn't have been able to fall asleep, if there was really a chance we weren't going to make it!

Good thing for the disciples I'm not Jesus, as He handled it with a bit more grace than I would have.

> *Then He arose and rebuked the wind, and said to the sea, "Peace, be still!" And the wind ceased and there was a great calm. But He said to them, "Why are you so fearful? How is it that you have no faith?"*
>
> Mark 4:39-40

Okay, so maybe Jesus *was* a little grumpy they woke Him from His nap! Yet, His point is valid. The Son of God was in the boat with them! He had said they were going to the other side. But they didn't understand or believe, so they looked at their circumstances, became afraid, and even questioned His love for them.

The Cares of This World

The first of the thorns that choke the Word that we discussed earlier was the lust for other things. The second was the deceitfulness of riches. Now we have come to the third thorn: the cares of this world.

The storm that threatened to sink the disciples' boat could certainly be considered a care of this world, right? There are many other kinds of cares that can distract us: paying our bills, doing well in our studies, being successful in our careers, navigating relationships, facing health challenges—the list could go on and on.

The truth is, we will face negative circumstances throughout our lives. There is literally no way to avoid them because we live in a fallen world that has been corrupted by sin. Jesus even told us to expect them:

> *These things I have spoken to you, that in Me you may have peace. In the world you will have tribulation....*
>
> John 16:33

Gee, thanks, Jesus, what a promise! But we can't stop there! If we did, there could be a reason for us to lose hope and question His love for us. The rest of the verse is key:

> *...but be of good cheer, I have overcome the world.*
>
> John 16:33

Jesus is saying, "Yeah, you're going to face storms in this life. But do *not* let them steal your joy, because I have already won the victory for you! All you have to do to walk in that victory is believe in Me."

> *For whatever is born of God overcomes the world. And this is the victory that has overcome the world— our faith. Who is he who overcomes the world, but he who believes that Jesus is the Son of God?*
>
> 1 John 5:4-5

When we face tribulations and things don't seem to be changing, it's tempting to fall for the lie that God doesn't care and He isn't working on our behalf. But questioning God's love for us is a lie and temptation that comes directly from the spirit of mammon.

You see, mammon's whole design is to stop you from trusting God and to trust in the things of the world instead. The goal is to deceive you into taking your eyes off the Lord and to serve mammon instead—because you can't serve two masters. You can be loyal to the one and despise the other, but you cannot serve both (Matthew 6:24).

Don't Be Distracted

Let's see how this played out in Martha's life of serving Jesus:

> *Now it happened as they went that He entered a certain village; and a certain woman named Martha welcomed Him into her house. And she had a sister called Mary, who also sat at Jesus' feet and heard His word. But Martha was distracted with much serving, and she approached Him and said, "Lord, do You not care that my sister has left me to serve alone? Therefore tell her to help me."*

EXPOSING THE SPIRIT OF MAMMON

And Jesus answered and said to her, "Martha, Martha, you are worried and troubled about many things. But one thing is needed, and Mary has chosen that good part, which will not be taken away from her."

Luke 10:38-42

First, I want us to notice that Mary *also* sat at Jesus' feet. Both of these women were listening to His Word being taught. Yet, it says Martha got distracted.

This word is the Greek *perispaó,* and it means "to draw away." Martha was drawn away from listening at Jesus' feet by her natural responsibilities of serving the people who were visiting her home.

How many people would do the same thing if there were people in their home? You'd want to make sure there was enough food, the plates stocked, the cutlery available, and drinks for anyone thirsty.

But not only did she become distracted, Martha then noticed she was all alone in the work she was doing. She got a bit perturbed that her little sister wasn't helping, so she complained to Jesus about it.

...Lord, do You not care that my sister has left me to serve alone? Therefore tell her to help me.

Luke 10:40

This word *care* here is the same Greek word used in Mark 4:38 by the disciples when they were in the storm with Jesus. It is the Greek word *meló,* and it means a "care, an object of anxiety, or something to be concerned with."

"Jesus, don't You care about me? Don't You love me? Don't You share my worry or concern?"

Nope! He's resting! He isn't worried about a thing because He has 100 percent faith that the Father is taking care of things for Him.

> *And Jesus answered and said to her, "Martha, Martha, you are worried and troubled about many things. But one thing is needed, and Mary has chosen that good part, which will not be taken away from her."*
>
> Luke 10:41-42

Jesus pointed out that Martha had been distracted by mammon, by the cares of this world, and it had gotten her worried and busy trying to serve. So much so that she wasn't listening to Him anymore.

What was the good part? Mary's eyes were fixed on Jesus. The only voice she was listening to was the voice of God. She wasn't concerned at all with what was going on in the natural around her because the Word of God, flowing from Jesus' mouth, was her number-one focus and priority.

> *You will keep him in perfect peace, whose mind is stayed on You, because he trusts in You.*
>
> Isaiah 26:3

I can hear the questions now: *"But Ashley, how were these people supposed to get fed and cared for if Martha didn't do it?"* Well, when there were 5,000 men, plus women and children, who were hungry in the wilderness, He miraculously provided for them with five loaves and two fish!

If we will simply sit at Jesus' feet, He will give us instruction on how to take care of the natural things. He will say, "Go take that job interview; start that business; move to that city." He'll tell us what to do, but we must remain seated at Jesus' feet, listening to His Word.

If we get distracted and start taking on the burden for looking after our families, paying the bills, and doing everything in our own strength, it will draw us away from our relationship with God. We will end up spinning our wheels, frustrated, and burnt out, lose the joy of the Lord, and will no longer be able to hear God's voice clearly.

Do Not Worry

Worry is just another word for the cares of this world. It is mammon's ploy to draw us away from God's voice. If God tells us to do something and we question our own ability to take care of these things—"How am I gonna pay the rent; how will I make the car payment; how am I going to put the kids through college?"—we are listening to the wrong voice!

> No one can serve two masters; for either he will hate the one and love the other, or else he will be loyal to the one and despise the other. You cannot serve God and mammon.
>
> Therefore I say to you, do not worry about your life, what you will eat or what you will drink; nor about your body, what you will put on. Is not life more than food and the body more than clothing? Look at the birds of the air, for they neither sow nor reap nor gather into barns; yet your heavenly Father feeds them. Are you not of more value than they? Which of you by worrying can add one cubit to his stature?

So why do you worry about clothing? Consider the lilies of the field, how they grow: they neither toil nor spin; and yet I say to you that even Solomon in all his glory was not arrayed like one of these. Now if God so clothes the grass of the field, which today is, and tomorrow is thrown into the oven, will He not much more clothe you, O you of little faith?

Therefore do not worry, saying, "What shall we eat?" or "What shall we drink?" or "What shall we wear?" For after all these things the Gentiles seek. For your heavenly Father knows that you need all these things. But seek first the kingdom of God and His righteousness, and all these things shall be added to you."

Matthew 6:24-33

When Jesus said, "do not worry," the word *worry* is the Greek word *merimnaó*. That word means "to be anxious or distracted, to go to pieces because of being pulled apart in different directions, dividing and fracturing a person's being into parts."

This is why Jesus emphasized in this passage that we shouldn't worry. Worry takes our eyes off of Jesus and puts them onto the circumstances, which can only result in defeat.

Jesus specifically directs us to think about the birds that don't sow or reap or maintain a growing savings account. As believers, we are great about this: "I'm sowing and reaping, I'm saving, and I'm believing for my needs to be met."

I teach on finances, and I believe in the power of sowing and reaping. However, if you are taking on the burden of that, trying to make it happen yourself, for providing for your needs through your own sowing and reaping, then you've gone full circle and you're back to listening to mammon. You're having an assurance in your own resources, which is the pride of life.

Rather than trusting in your own sowing and reaping, saving, good financial decisions—and even in your own faith— you must trust in God. God is going to supply your needs!

Consider the lilies: they don't spin thread and sew clothing, yet they are dressed better than the richest man in all of human history! Jesus is basically saying, "Which of you, by worrying, can do anything productive?" Nothing good comes from worry. It only divides our attention to draw us away from keeping our eyes on Jesus.

So, do not worry! Sit at Jesus' feet first—listen to His Word— and all these earthly needs (clothes, food, mortgage, car payment, etc.) will be added to you as well.

God is our loving Father. He takes care of His kids. If you are taking on the burden as if God might not take care of you, you are listening to the voice of mammon, and it will block your relationship with God.

5

HEARING GOD'S VOICE

In the first part of this book, I exposed the tricks the spirit of mammon plays. We learned how the voice of mammon uses the lust of the flesh, the lust of the eyes, and the pride of life to deceive us into trusting in natural resources rather than the Lord. Following God's voice, trusting in Him, and placing His direction as our top priority will result in avoiding those money traps.

So we know what the voice of mammon sounds like, and we know following God's voice is the best way. But how do we hear the voice of God? What does God's voice sound like? How can we know that we are following His lead rather than the voice of mammon?

There are certainly challenges to hearing God's voice, but they nearly always come down to our focus. Are we focusing on the world, or are we focusing on the truth found in the Word? When our eyes are on Jesus, we can learn to tune in to the Father's voice and hear Him more clearly.

You Can Hear God

I can't tell you the number of times my wife Carlie and I have heard people say to us, "I can't hear God speaking to me. I've tried to read the Bible, I've tried to sit still and listen, but no matter what I do, I just can't hear God speaking to me!"

But what does the Bible say about this?

My sheep hear My voice, and I know them, and they follow Me.

John 10:27

Jesus is very clear in this passage. If you belong to Jesus, you *can* hear His voice! The biggest obstacle in hearing God's voice is right between your ears. You may have these, or similar, thoughts: *I can't hear God. He's a spiritual being and doesn't use an audible voice. There's no way I can actually hear Him speaking to me. People who say they hear God talk to them are crazy: they are hearing voices!*

These are all lies from the pit of hell, intended to keep you separated from communicating with the God who created you! God wants to speak to you. In fact, He is *always* speaking to you.

Wi-Fi and cellular signals are constantly streaming in the air around you, but you can't take advantage of them unless you have a device that is connected. By believing and confessing the lie that you can't hear God's voice, you are allowing your own mind to block the signal!

The first step in beginning to tune in to God's frequency and hear His voice is to believe you can and confess, "I am a child of God. I am one of His sheep, and I *do* hear His voice. I follow Him!" As you begin to take that step, you will start hearing Him more often and more clearly. It may even surprise you how easy it is.

It is fundamental to recognize, believe, and confess that as a child of God, He does speak to you and you can and do hear His voice. God wants you to hear Him even more than you do. Your ability to hear Him and follow His voice is vital to living the victorious Christian life in every area, not just escaping the traps of mammon.

> *But he who is joined to the Lord is one spirit with Him.*
>
> 1 Corinthians 6:17

When you gave your heart to Jesus and became born again, your spirit became one with God's Spirit. You became brand-new. Even though your flesh and your mind remained the same, your spirit was reborn with a direct line of communication with God!

When God speaks to us, this is where that communication takes place: spirit to Spirit. He doesn't pop up physically to sit on the couch for a chat! Now, this certainly *could* happen, but it's not the most common way that God communicates with us.

There are many ways the Lord can speak to us, but regardless of the method, it is always spirit to Spirit. This is why the Bible tells us that spiritual things are foolishness to the natural mind (1 Corinthians 2:14). However, as a born-again believer, you are able to fully comprehend spiritual things—not through your natural mind or logic, but by the Spirit.

The Spirit of God speaks to our spirits in a way we can easily understand. That is why many times we miss it! It is such an obvious, simple thing we can easily discount as being our "imagination," when really it is the Lord trying to get through to us.

When the Lord speaks to you, because it is through your spirit, the "voice" can sound like your own. He doesn't speak in King James! He won't usually say, "Thus saith the Lord of hosts!"

No, when God speaks, it is that still, small voice. It may be a random thought that pops in out of nowhere. It could be a revelation you have while reading your Bible. It could be an answer to a question that comes to mind as you pray in the spirit.

Regardless of the method, don't discount it if it comes easily. Relationship with God is not complicated!

Let's read something else Jesus said about us hearing God's voice:

> No longer do I call you servants, for a servant does not know what his master is doing; but I have called you friends, for all things that I heard from My Father I have made known to you.
>
> John 15:15

Jesus said that He calls us His friends! The relationship between friends isn't one of servant and master. God isn't sitting on His throne, bossing us around, tossing orders out with the threat, "Do this, or else!"

The relationship we have with Jesus is one of a deep, abiding friendship. This verse even says that because of this friendship, Jesus makes known to us everything the Father God makes known to Him. He wants you to hear every direction, every bit of wisdom, and every word of love He is speaking to you.

It takes a conscious and deliberate decision to begin to grow in your sensitivity to God's voice. Most importantly, however, it takes faith! If you are going to hear Him speak to you, you must believe that He wants to and that when He does, you *will* hear Him.

God Speaks through His Word

The most important way God speaks to us is through His Word. Any other way God speaks is good, of course, but there is no more sure way of hearing God's voice than by reading the Bible. The wisdom found within is timeless, perfect, and applicable to our lives today. God will use the Scriptures to lead and guide you, to teach you how to live victoriously and make wise decisions throughout your life.

Your word is a lamp to my feet and a light to my path.
Psalm 119:105

The Word of God is much more than just a book! John 1:14 tells us that Jesus is the Word of God made flesh. God spoke this universe into existence, and Jesus was also spoken into existence through every word of prophecy throughout the Old Testament. Jesus is the Word, and the Word is alive and full of power (Hebrews 4:12)!

Proverbs 6:22 says, *"When you roam, they* [the Scriptures] *will lead you; when you sleep, they will keep you; and when you awake, they will speak with you."* The Word of God will speak with you! It is actually one of the clearest ways God will communicate with you.

However, you have to actually read the Word for it to speak to you! If you have fifteen different Bible versions, but they all stay on a shelf, unopened, the life within them will not benefit you. You must open it up and feed on the Word of God regularly—ideally daily!

Don't read the Bible as if it is just a novel. Invite the Holy Spirit to reveal the Word to you as you read it. He will help you understand the truth within and how to apply it to your life.

For the word of God is living and powerful, and sharper than any two-edged sword, piercing even to the division of soul and spirit, and of joints and marrow, and is a discerner of the thoughts and intents of the heart.

Hebrews 4:12

What does it mean that the Word is alive? Does that mean that it changes its meaning? Not at all! Whatever Scripture says, its meaning will not change over time. Since God doesn't change, neither does His Word. However, you can read the Bible over and over again and each time discover something new. The Holy Spirit can reveal something you have never seen before.

There also may be times when you are seeking a specific answer from the Lord. As you read the Bible, a passage may come alive to you, giving you guidance in your situation, even though it may be a different circumstance from what was taking place when it was written.

For example, you have been praying about whether or not to take a job in another city. In Joshua 1:2, you read, *"Now therefore, arise, go...to the land which I am giving to them."* Your heart leaps, and somehow, deep inside, you *know* that the Lord is confirming that you are to go, although not specifically to Israel, as God was telling Joshua in that verse.

The Word is alive, and although the meaning hasn't changed, He can use certain passages to lead and guide you. When God speaks this way, it is called a *rhema* word. As it describes in Hebrews 4:12, it feels as though the Word pierces your heart like a knife! You know in the depths of your heart that God just used His Word to speak to you.

All Scripture is given by inspiration of God, and is profitable for doctrine, for reproof, for correction, for instruction in righteousness.

2 Timothy 3:16

God gave us the Bible to use in our everyday lives. It reveals who Jesus is, the nature and character of God, gives us wisdom, guides us, and teaches us the way we should go. There are many scriptures that emphasize the importance of the Word of God.

Yet I've heard some people say, "Oh, I don't read the Word; I just listen to God." This is foolishness! If you don't know what the Word says, it will be very easy to be led astray because you won't have a solid foundation. The Word is what helps you decipher whether what you are hearing is God's voice, your voice, the voice of mammon, or some other voice.

For example, I met a young man once—married with young children—who said the Lord told him he didn't need to work because God would provide for them. So, he wasn't even trying to find a job. This young man thought he was hearing God's voice but failed to measure what he had "heard" against the Word of God.

For even when we were with you, we commanded you this: If anyone will not work, neither shall he eat.

2 Thessalonians 3:10

But if anyone does not provide for his own, and especially for those of his household, he has denied the faith and is worse than an unbeliever.

1 Timothy 5:8

There are many other verses that also confirm this point: God provides for us, yes, but one way He does that is through what you put your hands to (Deuteronomy 30:9). If you put your hands to nothing, there isn't anything for Him to bless and increase.

The voice we hear, desires we feel, provocations in our hearts, dreams we have, visions we see, or words from other people are not always so obviously opposed to the Word of God. However, the Bible is always our very first measuring stick to see if what we are hearing is from Him.

Jesus said that the Holy Spirit will guide us into all truth. When you read the Word, ask the Holy Spirit to reveal it to you. Be ready for Him to show you something new you've never seen, thought about, or understood before.

Hearing God Is Simple

The challenge many believers have in hearing God's voice is making it entirely too complicated! We think God must speak to us in an audible voice our natural ears can hear, or we want to have two dreams and a vision to confirm that what we are hearing is from God.

> *For as many as are led by the Spirit of God, these are sons of God.*
>
> Romans 8:14

But remember, we are one spirit with Him now (1 Corinthians 6:17). He doesn't usually speak in spectacular ways, although He certainly can. Most often, we miss His voice, or disregard it, because we think, *Oh, that must just be me. I made that up.*

But if God is speaking to you by His Spirit—Spirit to spirit, as His guidance comes through your spirit into your mind—His words will have your voice. When He speaks to you, many times it will sound exactly like you!

John 6:63 says, *"The Spirit alone gives eternal life. Human effort accomplishes nothing. And the very words I have spoken to you are spirit and life"* (NLT). The words Jesus speaks to us are spirit, not flesh. We won't be able to identify them through natural means.

So how do we know what we are hearing is the Lord and not our own natural thoughts? We've discussed the vital importance of making the Word our foundation. Therefore, the first test is to ask, "Does this violate the Word of God?"

Second, does what you are hearing confirm that God is love? Is it a thought of condemnation or of edification? Does the thought bring fear or encouragement?

If you have presented God a question, sometimes the answer comes later, hitting you out of the blue. Seemingly random thoughts can be an indication that God is speaking to you, not your imagination. So when you have thoughts out of the blue, test it against the Word and consider that the Lord may just be trying to tell you something!

A Matter of Life or Death

Hearing God's voice clearly isn't an optional part of the life of a believer. It can very possibly be a matter of life or death!

One day I was driving, and I saw a hitchhiker walking down the side of the road. I heard the still, small voice of the Lord say, "Pick up that hitchhiker." At first I thought, *No, that's just me,* because I really didn't want to! In fact, I even passed him by. But after I had passed, it was like the Holy Spirit was yelling at me to pick him up! So I made a U-turn and went back for him.

After I started driving, he asked me, "So, what do you do for a living?"

I answered, "I'm a minister."

He looked at me and said, "Are you kidding me? Just two minutes ago I prayed and said, 'God, send someone to help me. I need one of Your workers to help me!'"

We spent about 20 minutes together. He had been born again years ago, but he rededicated his life to the Lord. I also led him in the baptism of the Holy Spirit, and he received his prayer language. It was a powerful time of ministry!

When I dropped him off, he got out of my truck and said, "I want you to know, this was going to be my last night. I was going to end everything tonight. I prayed today, and I said, 'God, if You love me, You're going to have to show me.' And spending time with you today has really encouraged me—I feel like a new man now!"

He had started off beaten down and considering suicide, but he left encouraged and ready go live life!

While we were still living in England, my wife, Carlie, had been practicing hearing the voice of God. One day, while at her computer, she heard the Lord say, "The cat is eating your pie." Seeing all three of our cats in the room with her, she disregarded the voice as being her imagination. After the third time, however, she figured she should check it out!

Reaching the kitchen, she found a stray cat had come in through the window and—sure enough—was eating her freshly baked pie! While this situation wasn't life or death, it helped train her to identify the voice of God for a much more serious situation.

A few days later, Carlie was driving down the hedge-lined country lane with the children, when she heard inside of her, "Brake!" She didn't question it and responded immediately. Out of a hidden farm gate in front of them, another vehicle shot out into the road! Listening to the Lord probably saved the lives of my family!

Practice hearing the Lord speak to you in the little moments to prepare you for more important situations. Hearing God's voice clearly can be a matter of life or death: for you and for others.

An Audible Voice

Most often, the Lord doesn't speak to us in an audible voice recognized through our natural ears. However, it can happen, and it usually is in cases of extreme importance.

When I was 16 years old, my mother and sister had given their lives to the Lord, but I was still very rebellious against the things of God. I thought it was all made up and didn't want to hear about Jesus in any way!

However, one night I woke up in the middle of the night to a voice saying, "Ashley!" This happened four or five times throughout the night, and after the first few times, I finally figured out it was the voice of God calling me into relationship with Him.

The next morning when I woke up, I gave my life to Jesus!

Some people will say, "Oh, you've heard the audible voice of God? That must mean you are really special!" But I think it's the opposite. If you hear the audible voice of God, it may be because you haven't been listening to Him speak to you in other ways and it was the only way He could get through to you!

Hearing the audible voice of God is rare, and we don't *need* it. Our relationship with God is based on faith. We walk by faith, not by sight (2 Corinthians 5:7), so our natural senses—including hearing—are not what we should rely on as believers.

The Bible is a more solid foundation than an audible voice from heaven. If you have never heard God's audible voice, you are probably among the majority of believers! You are not a sub-par Christian. Keep your eyes on Jesus and stay more in tune to hear that still, small voice speaking directly to your heart.

God Can Use Others

God can also use other people to speak into your life by a word of knowledge or wisdom, according to the Holy Spirit.

> *And finding disciples, we stayed there seven days. They told Paul through the Spirit not to go up to Jerusalem.*
>
> Acts 21:4

Another verse also refers to God using others to help you. Proverbs 27:17 says, *"As iron sharpens iron, so a man sharpens the countenance of his friend."* This method of sharpening blades requires two blades being sharpened by each other. Alone, each blade would remain dull!

In the same way, the Lord can use us to speak to one another words of encouragement, wisdom, or sometimes even correction. As members of the body of Christ, we need one another, and God often uses us in this way.

However, people are also imperfect and can unintentionally—and sometimes purposefully—allow the flesh to impact their words and behavior. Since we are aware of these dangers, we must always weigh what others say against what the Bible says. Remember, the Word is our foundation by which we measure everything!

For example, when Jesus told His disciples He had to die on the cross, Peter objected. He certainly didn't do this maliciously, but it violated what God the Father had told Jesus to do. Therefore, Jesus didn't follow what Peter said from his flesh. He moved forward with what the Word of God was to Him (Matthew 16:21-23).

God will usually use people to confirm something He has already said to you. When someone gives you a word, if it doesn't resonate with your spirit, put it on a shelf. It may be a confirmation for something later. Or you might need to disregard it. Sometimes people can get it wrong, but sometimes they get it right!

God Can Speak through Your Desires

Have you ever heard anyone teach that God speaks through your desires? Well, I believe that can be true! But before you decide to burn me at the stake for heresy, bear with me for just a bit.

> *Delight yourself also in the Lord, and He shall give you the desires of your heart.*
>
> Psalm 37:4

Sometimes the Lord *can* speak to you through your own desires. If you are in a solid relationship with the Lord, spending time with Him regularly and practicing hearing His voice, He will use your own desires to lead you. This verse doesn't mean that God will give you everything your flesh wants.

Instead, the Lord will place the desires He has for you within your heart so you will want the same things He wants.

When we are delighting in the Lord, our desires will mirror His own. We won't want to sin; we will want to do what pleases Him. When a fork in the road appears, our heart will not be to do what makes our flesh happy, but we will take the path that brings us true joy, which will often line up with His will.

Before the Lord spoke to my wife and me to launch our own ministry, we had no desire to do so! We were happy just to serve in another man's ministry and do what we could to support it.

However, when the Lord spoke to us to start Terradez Ministries, our desires changed! We began to *want* to launch our own ministry, even though we hadn't wanted to before.

While we were delighting ourselves in the Lord, we were exactly where He wanted us to be, working for someone else. But when He wanted us to move into a new arena of ministry, He changed our desires to match His own!

The word *delight* in this verse means to be soft or pliable. Delighting yourself in the Lord means to have a soft heart toward Him. Being pliable means you are surrendered to Him, allowing Him to change you. It doesn't mean doing everything perfectly.

However, no matter what, God is always there, eagerly anticipating time with you. Make communicating with Him part of your everyday life, and you will be able to trust the desires of your heart!

Trusting your desires to lead you can be a little nerve-racking. You have a sudden desire to go to the ice cream shop, but is it the Holy Spirit leading you or your flesh? How can you know if it's the Holy Spirit, you, or a temptation?

*After they had come to Mysia, they tried to go into
Bithynia, but the Spirit did not permit them.*

Acts 16:7

In this verse, Paul and his company tried to go into a certain region to minister, but the Holy Spirit turned them back. Many times when we are faced with a decision, we end up immobilized by indecision. Is it the Lord? Or is it the flesh? We wonder sometimes even if the enemy is trying to trick us into making the wrong decision.

However, most of the time the worst thing we can do is nothing at all. Usually, there is a step we can take to move forward that isn't going to "close the deal." If you feel led toward making a certain decision, but you aren't sure it's from the Lord, go ahead and take a small step. That step may be as simple as writing your decision down.

After you have taken that first step, consult with the Lord again. Colossians 3:15 tells us to let the peace of God rule in our hearts. If you feel peace regarding that step, take another! Follow the peace of God.

If the direction you are going is *not* God, He will let you know! It may be an unsettled feeling. A lack of peace. Just like in this verse, Paul started to go to Bithynia, but the Holy Spirit let him know he was going in the wrong direction, so he changed course. However, you can't steer a parked car! In order for the Lord to direct you, you usually first have to get moving.

Using the ice cream shop example, get in the car and start driving. If you have missed it, and it's just your flesh that wants ice cream, you'll begin to feel conviction from the Holy

Spirit. On the other hand, you might be surprised to feel peace, instead. God may be setting you up for a divine appointment!

> *Now while Paul waited for them at Athens, his spirit was provoked within him when he saw that the city was given over to idols.*
>
> Acts 17:16

What does it feel like when your spirit is provoked? In this verse, the word *provoked* means "to sharpen or stimulate." It basically means that the Spirit of God provoked Paul's spirit and stimulated his emotions, in this case a righteous anger, which caused him to take action.

In a similar way, the Spirit of God can provoke your spirit as well. Perhaps it is a righteous anger in the face of injustice, or compassion for the poor. You might feel a stirring in your spirit to do something to help abused women or in support of unwed mothers.

Maybe you feel the Lord calling you to write music or books, travel the world as a missionary, or attend Bible school. The Lord will provoke your spirit to do what He is calling you to do.

When I was trying to sell our house in England, I was coming against multiple obstacles that seemed insurmountable. One of these challenges was that the tenants in this house were a wonderful Christian family who had been renting from us for more than ten years. I felt the Lord tell me to put people before profit, so we knew we didn't want to sell the home out from under them.

As I prayed about the situation, the Lord prompted me to attend a specific business conference. He told me, "When you get there, this specific friend will have your answer."

I trusted God and obeyed! When I got to the conference, I saw my friend and approached him. I explained the situation to him and told him God said he would have my answer. However, my friend didn't respond the way I had expected.

"Ashley," he said, "I'll give it some thought, but right now, I honestly have no idea what to tell you!"

I went to my hotel room a little confused. I knew God had spoken to me very specifically that my friend would have the answer, but he hadn't. What now? I continued to pray and felt peace about it. I felt the Lord confirm to me I had not missed His leading and to keep trusting. So, I did. I went to bed at peace, knowing God had my answer and it would come.

The next day, my friend excitedly approached me.

"Ashley! Come with me, there's someone I need to introduce you to!"

He led me to an English woman. He had just met her that morning, and they began to tell me her side of the story.

She had been praying to the Lord for an investment property to buy in England. Her requirements were very specific in regard to the number of beds and baths, within a certain distance of her home. She also told the Lord that she didn't want to advertise, but to find something that didn't need renovation and already had established tenants! As she had been praying, God had told her to attend this conference in the United States! She trusted God and had come all the way from England.

When my friend heard her story, he immediately realized, "Ashley was right! I do have his answer right here in front of me!"

My property was *exactly* what she had been praying for! The deal we made was a win-win-win! She got her investment property, without having to renovate or find tenants, the current family didn't have to find a new place to live, and we got to sell without having to advertise. As a bonus, we were able to continue storing all our English possessions in the garage free of charge!

As we prayed and believed God, giving this situation into His hands, God sent both of us to a conference where we would cross paths. He had even known in advance that my friend would be the one to make our connection.

God is the most amazing strategist! He created this entire universe, in all its incredible complexities, and He knows the beginning from the end. He sees our past, present, and future. His ways are higher than our ways, and when we ask Him for guidance, listen to His voice, and then obey, truly miraculous results will come to pass in our lives!

6

BECOMING ALPHA DOG

Breaking the power of the spirit of mammon over your life takes consistent effort. It takes daily focus of recognizing its voice and choosing to listen to the voice of God instead. This isn't a one-time step. We have to assert dominance over the spirit of mammon every day.

Just like my little puppy, either you are leading your finances, or your finances are leading you. If you allow it, the spirit of mammon will lead you into a lifestyle of lack rather than plenty. You must become alpha dog over your finances!

There are several ways you can assert dominance over your finances and shut the mouth of the spirit of mammon.

First, stay thankful for everything God has already done and given you. Thankfulness shuts the mouth of covetousness and enables you to continue to receive increase from the Lord.

Second, listen to and believe the voice of God. If the Word of God says you are blessed, believe it! Stay sensitive to God's voice and be humble enough to receive it as the truth. His direction will always be best for you, even if it doesn't seem like it in the natural.

Third, give with a willing, generous, and joyful heart! When you give, you are directing your heart to the things of God, worshipping Him, and denying the deception of mammon. Giving also is planting seed for you to receive a harvest as well.

An Attitude of Gratitude

It's very easy to be thankful when everything is going well: when you have more money than month, there's extra to spend on eating out or going to the movies, when you have enough to give extra to your church or other ministries you want to support.

But what about when it seems like everything is going wrong? When the car breaks down, your coworker was promoted ahead of you, or you've lost your job altogether? When we are in the middle of a trial, it is a time when we *least* feel like praising God and giving thanks.

However, these moments are precisely the *most* important times to enter into thanksgiving and praise! In these moments of weakness, when you are under attack, the spirit of mammon will scream the loudest for you to pay attention to the problem rather than your solution.

Your attitude of thanksgiving—praising God in the midst of a trial—is exactly what you need to do in order to break the power of mammon in your situation, even when it looks like all is lost and there is no hope.

If you focus on what is happening around you, that is all you will see. Your focus on the negative becomes so narrow, it leaves no room for God to work! When you look to God, the One who provides your help, and give Him your praise and attention, He can move on your behalf.

> *Rejoice always, pray without ceasing, in everything give thanks; for this is the will of God in Christ Jesus for you.*
>
> 1 Thessalonians 5:16-18

Notice this scripture passage says to give thanks in every-thing, but not for everything. God doesn't allow or cause terrible things to happen to you. We live in a fallen world that has been corrupted by sin, so sometimes bad things happen, even to good, godly people. So you don't have to thank God *for* something awful that happens in your life!

However, you *can* stay thankful in the middle of a trial. When bad things happen, remember all the wonderful things God has already done for you! You are born again; you have a relationship with your Creator, who died so you could live in victory in this life. There are so many things to be thankful for, even when a storm comes.

There is a moment in the life of David that gives us an incredible example of looking to God for encouragement and help in the middle of a terrible circumstance.

In 1 Samuel 30, the Amalekites had raided the city of Ziklag and burned it. They had kidnapped the wives and children of all of David's men, including his own wives. His soldiers, who previously had been loyal to him, were so distraught and angry, they actually threatened to stone him because of it.

David was having a very bad day! Yet, in verse 6, it says, *"But David strengthened Himself in the Lord his God."* The King James Version translates it a little differently by saying that David *"encouraged Himself in the Lord."*

You can also encourage and strengthen yourself in the Lord through thanksgiving and praise! When you do so, this enables the Lord to come in and change your situation around.

As David was encouraged in the Lord, God told him, *"Pursue* [the Amalekite army], *for you shall surely overtake them and without fail recover all"* (1 Samuel 30:8). The inter-esting thing is that David's army of 400 men must have been vastly outnumbered, for it says in verse 17, *"Then David attacked them from twilight until the evening of the next day. Not a man of them escaped, except four hundred young men who rode on camels and fled."*

The number of the enemy who *ran away* from the fight was the same number of men David had to begin with!

> *So David recovered all that the Amalekites had carried away, and David rescued his two wives. And nothing of theirs was lacking, either small or great, sons or daughters, spoil or anything which they had taken from them; David recovered all.*
>
> 1 Samuel 30:18-19

David could have fallen apart, and said, "Oh, God! It's all over!" Instead, he found strength and encouragement by keeping his eyes on the Lord. Then God gave him instructions and—even against overwhelming odds—he recovered every person and possession that had been stolen!

Thanksgiving and Praise Brings Breakthrough

Let's look at one more example of where praise and thanksgiving can bring change to your situation.

In Acts 16, magistrates had torn off Paul and Silas' clothes, beaten them, and thrown them in prison. Even in a dark dungeon, backs beaten and feet in stocks, they did not moan and groan about their circumstances. They didn't say, "God! We were doing what You told us to do; how could You allow this to happen?"

Instead, the Bible tells us they kept their eyes on the Lord and praised Him.

But at midnight Paul and Silas were praying and singing hymns to God, and the prisoners were listening to them. Suddenly there was a great earthquake, so that the foundations of the prison were shaken; and immediately all the doors were opened and everyone's chains were loosed.

Acts 16:25-26

The chains in your life can be broken through the power of thanksgiving and praise! Magnify the good in your life, praise God, and give Him thanks in everything. There will always be something good that you can find to give thanks for! As you focus on the good, on how good God is, and rejoice in all things, you will experience breakthrough in your life.

Sometimes you may have to give the Lord thanks through gritted teeth when you're having a flesh-flash! Your flesh won't always enjoy what is going on because it is focused entirely on the natural realm: what you can see, taste, hear, smell, and feel.

Your carnal (natural or fleshly) nature might get upset when something bad happens in your life. Yet, your spirit is constantly rejoicing, and it is vital that you tap into that power and allow it to influence your soul. When you allow your spirit to dominate your soul, it makes all the difference!

Listen and Believe You Are Blessed

While attending Bible college, I had a side business of buying and selling cars. However, at one point, all of the money was tied up in the vehicles that hadn't yet sold. We didn't even have any cash to buy groceries!

The cars weren't selling, and Carlie was at the point where she was starting to grumble and complain. She had neglected to be thankful for what we had, only focusing on what was going wrong, and it was hindering our prosperity, having physical consequences.

She asked the Lord what was going on, and God told her, *"You've forgotten that you are blessed."* That was a wake-up call! Carlie changed her attitude, and rather than complaining about the lack, she thanked God for what we had. Then she laid hands on the cars and spoke blessings over each one. Within about three days, all the cars had sold!

Don't forget you're blessed! God has commanded a blessing over you, and there is nothing the enemy can do or say to change that!

I love the story of Balaam and his donkey in the book of Numbers. It's a long and complex story, but I'll give you a quick summary.

Balaam was a prophet, and the king of Moab, Balak, had asked him to curse the Israelites for him. Balaam was *really* tempted because Balak had said he would basically do *anything* Balaam wanted, if he would curse the Israelites for him!

So although Balaam initially rejected Balak's offer, he asked the Lord one more time, hoping God would say yes! Surprisingly, the Lord told Him, *"If the men come to call you, rise and go with them; but only the word which I speak to you— that you shall do"* (Numbers 22:20).

Balaam took that as, "God said I can go!" because rather than waiting for the men to come to him, he got up the next morning and went with them. Balaam was very tempted with the deceitfulness of riches and the lust of other things and wasn't fully listening to the voice of God. He was running after the voice of mammon!

It says in verse 22 that God was angry with Balaam because he went, so he sent the Angel of the Lord to stand in his way. This is when the famous donkey did her best to save Balaam's life by withstanding his abuse and *speaking* to him!

I'd love to talk about this in more detail, but I don't want to get distracted from the point here. Please read Numbers 22-24. You'll see how often the voice of mammon was calling to Balaam and trying to seduce him into doing the wrong thing for financial gain. It's a fascinating read.

Ultimately, Balaam was corrected (by his own donkey, of all things) and realized he had been following the wrong voice. So he listened to God and finally told Balak what the Lord had wanted him to say. (Actually, it took multiple burnt offerings in multiple locations for Balaam to give all of his prophecies to Balak. He *really* wanted that money and was hoping God would let him curse the Israelites!)

> ...*Rise up, Balak, and hear! Listen to me, son of Zippor! God is not a man, that He should lie, nor a son of man, that He should repent. Has He said, and will He not do? Or has He spoken, and will He not make it good? Behold, I have received a command to bless; He has blessed, and I cannot reverse it.*
>
> Numbers 23:18-20

Do you see the message so clearly given here? First, God doesn't lie. His Word says you are blessed through your faith in Jesus! God will never repent, which means He will never change His mind about the blessing He has given you. If He has said it, He will do it! He always keeps His promises.

Guide Your Heart through Giving

The voice of mammon is loud, and it tries to get us to submit to the world's system. If we do things the way the world does, it will severely restrict how we can increase according to the economy of the Kingdom of God.

Remember how my little puppy was leading me, rather than me leading him? I had to become the alpha dog of my house, otherwise that little guy would completely take over! In the same way, we must become the alpha dog of our finances. One of the greatest ways to shut the mouth of mammon and assert dominance over our finances is through giving.

> *For where your treasure is, there your heart will be also.*
>
> Matthew 6:21

God has good things for us, and He wants us to have them, but He needs to be the number-one priority in our lives so we can receive them. He loves you so much and yearns for fellowship with you! He doesn't want to be second place to money!

We simply can't receive everything God has for us if He is even second place in our lives. He is a jealous God, and He wants all of our heart.

You may be thinking to yourself, *What are my priorities?* Well, I can tell very clearly what they are by simply looking at your spending habits. I know that seems harsh, but it is absolutely true. Are your children or grandchildren a priority? Are your hobbies a top priority? These things will show up in your spending.

You are probably already giving on a monthly basis to all sorts of things: entertainment streaming services, gym memberships, eating out, or daily coffee purchases. You're already giving, but you're giving to the things that matter to you the most. If your giving to other things overshadows your giving to the Kingdom of God, there may be an issue with where your heart is.

> *Hear, my son, and be wise; and guide your heart in the way.*
>
> Proverbs 23:19

You can actually guide your heart. How? First, by where you place your attention. As I stated earlier, if your focus is on your problems, those problems will only be magnified. However, with your eyes on Jesus, on the Word of God, the promises of God, and what God has said regarding your life—you will guide your heart in that direction instead.

Another way you can guide your heart is through giving. Where is your treasure? You can identify where your heart currently is by seeing where your treasure is. However, you can also intentionally guide your heart into God's direction through placing your physical treasure in His hands.

I've heard people say, "I want to love God more," or, "I just don't feel love for God like I think I should." If you want to love God more, give to guide your heart toward Him and the things He cares about. Give to help establish His Kingdom here on the earth. As you give, you will find your heart will follow!

> *No one can serve two masters; for either he will hate the one and love the other, or else he will be loyal*

to the one and despise the other. You cannot serve
God and mammon.

Matthew 6:24

This verse doesn't say you can't serve both God and the devil. That would be too easy! He said God and mammon—the spirit behind money. When you make God your focal point, you can't have mammon as your focal point at the same time. You can't have two priorities; it has to be one or the other. God or money.

Again, that doesn't mean we can't be wealthy! God *wants* us to be rich! He wants us to succeed and have an abundance. But in order to live in godly abundance, we must rely on God for our security and decision-making.

With your wisdom and your understanding you
have gained riches for yourself, and gathered gold
and silver into your treasuries; by your great wisdom
in trade you have increased your riches, and your
heart is lifted up because of your riches.

Ezekiel 28:4-5

This is what happens to your heart when you follow the voice of mammon regarding your finances. You can use all the natural wisdom you have to become rich, but it will result in nothing but pride and, ultimately, your downfall.

Honor the Lord with your possessions, and with the
firstfruits of all your increase; so your barns will be

filled with plenty, and your vats will overflow with new wine.

Proverbs 3:9-10

Putting God first place means we even give to Him the first of our increase! It seems like we go to church, we worship Him with music, and then when it comes offering time, we give Him a tip. It's like giving financially is an afterthought, not a primary method of our worship.

Your giving touches God's heart. He doesn't *want* or *need* your money! He owns the cattle on a thousand hills (Psalm 50:10). He is the Creator of the universe: He doesn't want your money; He wants your *heart*.

So often, we desire to give God our whole hearts, but struggle when it comes to giving of our finances. But when we give our best to Him, He is getting our whole heart! The result of our barns (bank accounts) being filled with plenty isn't because we somehow have fulfilled a requirement for giving. It is because when we give, our hearts are open to receive!

When you give, does that make God love you more? No! However, when your heart is moved toward God through giving, your love for Him grows. He opens the doors of heaven to pour out a blessing on you so great you can't even receive it all (Malachi 3:10), and you will gain fulfillment in a way only giving to the Kingdom can bring.

A Heart of Faith

Whether we are currently struggling financially or maybe doing great, both situations can still result in us following the voice of mammon rather than the voice of God regarding our finances. When we give, we are asserting our dominance and showing mammon that it isn't the strongest voice anymore.

Giving to God isn't really giving Him what is ours anyway; all we have already belongs to Him, and He has provided us seed to sow.

> Now may He who supplies seed to the sower, and bread for food, supply and multiply the seed you have sown and increase the fruits of your righteousness, while you are enriched in everything for all liberality, which causes thanksgiving through us to God.
>
> 2 Corinthians 9:10-11

God gives you the resources you need to give into the Kingdom, and He also meets your natural needs. When you sow the seed God gives you, which is His anyway, He will multiply it back to you. Then you will increase and have even more seed to sow!

Consider the very first time the Bible talks about bringing offerings to the Lord:

> And in the process of time it came to pass that Cain brought an offering of the fruit of the ground to the Lord. Abel also brought of the firstborn of his flock and of their fat. And the Lord respected Abel and his offering, but He did not respect Cain and his offering. And Cain was very angry, and his countenance fell.
>
> Genesis 4:3-5

People often wonder why God didn't accept Cain's offering. Some say, "Oh, Abel gave a blood offering, and Cain's offering was only vegetables." However, that doesn't make sense. If Cain was a farmer, why would he give livestock?

Verse 3 uses the phrase, "in the process of time" Cain brought his offering. That phrase means, "at the end of the days." Basically, after everything was done, Cain finally got around to bringing God an offering. But Abel brought the *first-born* of his flock. Cain gave to God the last, but Abel gave the first.

Abel didn't know if there would be a second, third, or fourth. But his heart was focused on God, and he put Him in first place. Therefore, God accepted Abel's offering, not only for the gift itself but also because it reflected Abel's heart toward God.

Hebrews 11:6 tells us that without faith it is impossible to please God. And giving takes faith! If you're an adrenaline junky, giving can sometimes get your heart pumping harder than anything else!

Once I was invited to a mission's banquet to support a specific missionary. The hall was set up to receive 200 guests, but due to a snowstorm, only about 10 people showed up! I was asked to take up the offering. I did so, and I gave myself, too.

As I left, I was praying in the spirit, and I heard the Lord speak to me. He told me to take the $10,000 I had in savings for a home and give it all to this missionary.

At first, I plugged my ears and again said, "I can't hear You, Lord!" My flesh was having a hard time. Mammon was saying, "You've saved up so long for this. This money is for your home. How will you afford a down payment without this money you've worked so hard to save?" Let me tell you, it was talking loudly to me.

You know, our flesh doesn't like to listen to the voice of God, sometimes. I challenge you to pray in tongues for an extended period of time. Your natural mind will tell you, "This isn't working. You're wasting time!" But it is your spirit praying to God's Spirit. It's far from a waste of time.

If you want to get into faith, pray in the Holy Ghost and give a bunch of money! It will drag you into faith, kicking and screaming. It's like dragging your flesh along like a fit-throwing toddler: Come on! We're getting into faith. It'll be good for you!

Or try fasting. Your flesh will freak out! By 10 o'clock in the morning, it'll start telling you, "We're gonna starve!" But this is yet another way of taking the alpha dog position over your flesh and allowing your spirit to be the master, instead.

At any rate, I told my wife, Carlie, what I felt the Lord say about giving our savings.

She asked, "Are you sure?"

"I'm about 90 percent sure."

"Well, if you think it's God, do it!"

The following day I called the missionary and asked to meet with him. As I handed him the check, he began to cry. (Honestly, as the check left my hands, I think I started to cry, too! I guess my flesh still wasn't 100 percent convinced.) This missionary was a Rhema Bible College graduate who had been believing God to build a Bible school in Myanmar, and he needed exactly that amount to complete the project! I was so glad I had listened to the Holy Spirit instead of the voice of mammon.

When I got back into my truck and started driving home, I started praising God for that Bible school and for the resulting perpetual seed that would continue to be sown, year after year. What a blessing to be part of something like that! I was just thanking Him, and the tangible presence of God filled my truck so strongly, I had to pull over.

I heard God say, "Thank *you*, Ashley. I've been trying to get people to give that amount to his Bible school for months, but you were the first one to obey." I was floored.

God reminded me of when Carlie and I would dream of writing checks for thousands of dollars to give into the Kingdom. At that time, we had no money, no heating, and we had to make tough decisions when grocery shopping—coffee or cereal! But we dreamt about giving big!

God said, "You were already hearing My heart, hearing Me speak to you in that area. You were preparing to hear Me tell you to give big! I speak to so many people, but their hearts aren't with Me so they can't hear Me in that area."

It is a sobering thought to think of all the people God had spoken to first who either hadn't been able to hear or who had allowed mammon to talk them out of giving. Even my natural mind told me that the money we had saved was gone after we had given it.

Yet, our spirits knew it was only seed planted. And sure enough, soon after Carlie and I made this sacrificial gift, we were able to supernaturally buy the home we had been saving for with cash—completely debt-free!

God Notices Giving

Cornelius was a devout man who gave generously. Even this Gentile was noticed by God, and he was blessed as a result:

There was a certain man in Caesarea called Corne-lius, a centurion of what was called the Italian Regi-ment, a devout man and one who feared God with all his household, who gave alms generously to the people, and prayed to God always. About the ninth hour of the day he saw clearly in a vision an angel of God coming in and saying to him, "Cornelius!" And when he observed him, he was afraid, and said, "What is it, lord?" So he said to him, "Your prayers and your alms have come up for a memorial before God."

Acts 10:1-4

God noticed that Cornelius had a heart toward Him. Cornelius gave financially, and he prayed to God. Then God told him to send for Peter. Meanwhile, Peter had a vision to pre-pare him for Cornelius' servants to come request his presence.

Because of this divine connection, Cornelius was born again and baptized with the Holy Spirit. But not only him! The Bible tells us that there were *many* who had come together to hear what Peter had to say (Acts 10:27). In fact, this pas-sage is so important for those of us who are Gentiles, as Cornelius (along with the Ethiopian eunuch Philip ministered to in Acts 8:26-39) was one of the first Gentiles to be converted to Christianity.

This powerful moment in church history happened because a man, not of the Jewish faith or heritage, prayed to God con-sistently and gave generously!

Another time, Jesus was at the temple, watching as people gave into the treasury:

And He looked up and saw the rich putting their gifts into the treasury, and He saw also a certain poor widow putting in two mites. So He said, "Truly I say to you that this poor widow has put in more than all; for all these out of their abundance have put in offerings for God, but she out of her poverty put in all the livelihood that she had."

Luke 21:1-4

Jesus noticed how these people were giving. It wasn't really about how *much* people were giving. He noticed their hearts. This widow woman had her heart so much focused on the Lord she gave everything. She truly gave her entire heart to the Lord. And He saw it!

The Bible doesn't tell us what happened to that widow woman, but I truly don't believe that was the end of her story! I imagine one day we will be able to ask her in person, but I know in my heart she was blessed beyond measure.

But this I say: He who sows sparingly will also reap sparingly, and he who sows bountifully will also reap bountifully. So let each one give as he purposes in his heart, not grudgingly or of necessity; for God loves a cheerful giver. And God is able to make all grace abound toward you, that you, always having all sufficiency in all things, may have an abundance for every good work.

2 Corinthians 9:6-8

God loves a cheerful giver! It's not the same as when you give because you were manipulated into giving. When I teach giving, I never want those to whom I am speaking to think I am only after their money! In truth, I feel the same way Paul did when he wrote to the Philippian church:

> *Not that I seek the gift, but I seek the fruit that abounds to your account.*
>
> Philippians 4:17

To emphasize my point, I say this often and I will say it again here: If you have any doubt about my motivations in teaching you to give, please don't give to Terradez Ministries! Pray to the Lord and ask Him where He wants you to give and follow His leading, but please, give cheerfully and in faith!

Once my wife and I were ministering at a conference in a hotel ballroom in Atlanta. Our team had forgotten to send offering envelopes, so I thought to myself, *No problem. Our ministry is blessed. We don't need to take up an offering, so we will just skip it this time.*

The Lord immediately rebuked me! He said, "Do you think the offering is about your ministry receiving money? It's much more important to give people the opportunity to give!"

So, we obeyed the Lord. We got some plain envelopes from the hotel and received an offering. This led to multiple powerful testimonies of supernatural increase in the following days! We gave the audience the chance to give into the Kingdom, and they received a harvest as a result.

Again, God loves a cheerful giver. Sometimes when you give, you might feel like crying—like I did when we gave our savings—but give generously with joy! That word *cheerful* is the Greek word *hilaros*. Give hilariously! Be a prompt-to-do-it giver, joyfully, because you know it isn't God trying to take *from* you—He is trying to get so much more *to* you.

I've mentioned this before when sharing our testimony about Hannah's healing, but giving financially isn't a way to bribe God! He has already provided for you. He has already blessed you, and that blessing cannot be reversed!

But when we give, we are guiding our hearts in the way toward God. Our love for Him and faith in Him grows and we are more readily able to receive all of the provision, favor, and blessing He has already given to us.

It isn't, "Well, if I give more, I won't have to work. I can just give, and I will receive; men will give into my bosom (Luke 6:38)." That's not how it works! When you give cheerfully, generously, out of love and worship for God, then whatever you set your hand to will prosper. Yes, you will have favor and receive increase, but only if your heart is right!

> ...And remember the words of the Lord Jesus, that He said, "It is more blessed to give than to receive."
> Acts 20:35

Giving does change lives; and often when you give, the life changed the most is your own.

Recently we were raising money for our new Terradez Ministries headquarters. A friend of ours texted us one day and asked us how much we owed on the promissory note for the property. At the time we still owed a large sum of money. He responded that he would pay that off. Within a couple hours, he had made that transfer to us.

This was a sacrificial gift for this couple! It wasn't all they had, but it definitely took faith. However, they had a specific need in mind for which they were planting this seed.

They had been estranged from their adult child for five years. This person was an alcoholic and drug addict and had been in prison. They had only spoken to their child twice in the past five years and both times were not good experiences.

A couple of days after they gave this sacrificial gift, this prodigal child called them! Now out of prison, completely sober, there has been a complete turnaround! This family is now fully reconciled, and they are all serving the Lord.

The point of this story is your giving can bring you what money could never buy. This is similar to the story I told about when we gave financially and received Hannah's healing. Neither of us were giving to somehow bribe the Lord for the result we were believing for. God told us to give sacrificially, in a way that really required faith, and that moved us at a heart level to enable us to receive from God what He so deeply desired for us to have!

Not only can your giving bring you what money could never buy, when you give devotionally, God will also give back to you transactionally. What I mean by this is when you give from your heart out of love for God, His blessings will manifest—your home or investments increase in value, you get more work, you get a raise, people give to you, etc. So although we know by faith we will receive, we should be more excited about giving than receiving. Giving is fun!

Mammon Lies to Us about Giving

The bottom line is, when you give—even when your flesh or mammon tells you to do otherwise—you are asserting your dominance over your flesh and mammon. You are saying, "You are not the boss of me! I hear and obey God's voice, and I trust Him with my finances more than anyone or anything else."

Sometimes people have reasons why they don't give that sound good in the natural, or even holy. But mammon lies!

The spirit of mammon will use natural logic, or even spiritual-sounding reasons, to keep us from giving.

I've heard people say, "I only give when I feel led." What do they mean when they say "feel" led? Is it really a leading from their spirit, or are they letting their emotions, their flesh, dictate when they will give?

We can't always trust how we *feel*. Feelings are fickle and they can change on a dime. Most giving should actually be planned or committed ahead of time. I would estimate that 80 percent of my giving is to ministries and causes I have already committed to supporting.

Of course, the testimonies I have shared with you are from times the Lord has told me to give on the spur of the moment. However, those are the exceptions to my giving, not the rule! So beware of thinking to only give "when you feel led."

Another lie mammon will try to pass off as holy is to say, "I don't give money, I give time and prayers." Well, time and prayers are great, but we are also instructed to give financially. We can't use prayer and service as a substitution for giving.

However, if you are unable to give cheerfully, don't give up on the idea of giving altogether! You may want to go back to the beginning and say, "Lord, I realize my heart might not be right in this area. I want to guide my heart toward You by giving. So, I commit to give this amount every month. I don't feel cheerful about it right now, but I ask that You help this to guide my heart, soften my heart, and help me to grow in this grace of giving so that I can start to give hilariously to You!"

Another lie mammon will tell you is, "You can't afford to give." If you can't afford to give, that's the time when you most *need* to give! It's kind of like when we don't feel like worshipping or praising God is the most important time to start doing so. In fact, you can't afford *not* to give!

They say the definition of insanity is to do the same thing over and over and expect a different result. Our situations won't change unless we start doing something different. Sometimes that means praising and thanking the Lord when we don't feel like it, and sometimes that means giving financially into the Kingdom when we feel we don't have the money. Seed can't grow until it is planted into good soil!

Here is another lie you may hear mammon tell you, "I'll give when I have extra." Listen, if you won't give off ten dollars, you won't give off one hundred thousand dollars either. Even if you had "extra"—whatever that means—you still wouldn't give because you aren't used to giving now. Develop a habit of giving small, and then you will continue with that habit as you increase.

> For if there is first a willing mind, it is accepted according to what one has, and not according to what he does not have.
>
> 2 Corinthians 8:12

This scripture is talking about giving. Paul makes it very clear giving is based on what we have, not upon what we *don't* have. God will always give you *something* to sow. It doesn't have to be every penny you have (unless He specifically tells you to, and sometimes He might!), but give something from what you *do* have, and He will increase it. That is His promise, and He never breaks His word!

Have you heard this lie before? "I don't give to them because they don't need it." How do you know they don't need it? Most people who look to be doing very well financially, they are doing so because they are huge givers! When you give to them, they are then continuing to give to others, and the seed goes on and on.

A good friend of mine was criticized for having a new car. Someone said, "Instead of having that new car, you should give to missions!"

He responded, "You don't understand. The reason I *have* this new car is because I *have been* giving to missions. In fact, this car was given to me!"

Oftentimes, I choose to give to those who are very blessed because that blessing flows down. I want the favor and blessing they have! Sometimes I give to those who are doing well financially because I have learned something from them or been greatly blessed by their mentorship, wisdom, or revelation.

> *Those who are taught the word of God should provide for their teachers, sharing all good things with them.*
>
> Galatians 6:6 NLT

> *When we told the message to you, it was like planting spiritual seed. So we have the right to accept material things as our harvest from you.*
>
> 1 Corinthians 9:11 Contemporary English Version

Also remember to give where you are fed, as these verses teach us. If you're being fed by what they are teaching you, that's definitely a good work!

We don't give because of need. There is so much need in the world, we not only can't, but we shouldn't.

And God is able to make all grace abound toward you, that you, always having all sufficiency in all things, may have an abundance for every good work.

2 Corinthians 9:8

God's grace enables us to give to every *good* work, not every work! There are some things we shouldn't be giving money to, shouldn't be supporting. But many others we should! Listen to the Holy Spirit to show you which ground is good, which works are sharing the Gospel, helping the poor, expanding the Kingdom of God!

For example, Terradez Ministries doesn't only receive donations, we also give big! Missions and benevolent ministries are an important focus of our giving because we know Matthew 24:14 says the whole world must hear the Gospel before the end will come! Therefore, we give to multiple organizations located around the world. We know this is a wise investment to powerfully impact the lives of individuals and establish God's Kingdom and covenant here on earth (Deuteronomy 8:18).

You know, when the Queen of Sheba heard of Solomon's great wisdom, she came to him for him to teach her. She brought him an extravagant offering! Did Solomon need her wealth and riches? Of course not! He was the richest man alive. However, she gave as a way of showing honor, respect, and to give thanks.

In the same way, we give to the Kingdom of God. We do sometimes give to works that have need, and other times we give because we have been blessed and want to give back. We want to help spread the Gospel around the world. We give out of love for God. We give to plant seed. And we give to tell mammon to shut up and show who is alpha dog in our finances!

CONCLUSION

The temptations of the spirit of mammon are not new tricks. The devil has been using the same strategies he has used since the beginning of time. In fact, he fell for them, too! He was clothed in gold and precious stones (Ezekiel 28:12-17), but it wasn't enough for him. His greed and pride resulted in his own downfall.

The devil understands the temptation and distraction wealth—and lack—are to a believer. Thankfully, the Word of God has exposed his tricks to us, and we don't have to fall victim to them ever again!

The spirit of mammon is actively trying to pull you away from the Lord. It wants you to hear and obey its voice, thereby becoming your master instead of God. And as Jesus warned us, we cannot serve, love, and be loyal to two masters. We can only have one.

But now the deception has been exposed and you are fully equipped to recognize the voice of mammon for what it is! Knowledge is power, and now that you have read this book, you have the ability to see mammon's tactics for what they really are.

Now you can choose to turn everything around and speak to mammon with authority rather than listening to its voice.

Tell it what to do and where to go! Mammon must obey you now that God is in His rightful place as your Master.

Remember, money itself is not your enemy. We need money in this world, but we must ensure we make it our servant instead of allowing it to be our master. Money is a tool that can be used for either good or evil, and I believe you are more equipped now to use it for good.

Remember, you live in the natural world, but this world is not your true home! You are a child of the most high God, seated with Him in heavenly places (Ephesians 2:6). You are a spiritual being, and you have access to spiritual blessings that cause you to live a victorious, overcoming life here on earth. The spirit of mammon may try to get you to focus more on the natural realm, but if you stay in tune with God's perspective, you will stay clear of those traps.

Money will obey you as you obey the Lord!

EMPOWERING
BELIEVERS
IN THE
PROMISES
OF GOD

Ashley and Carlie Terradez are a power-packed duo, exercising Luke 4:18 by proclaiming and providing an example of God's promises and provision through Christ Jesus. With a special emphasis on relationship with God, supernatural healing, and financial provision, we empower people to access everything that Jesus has already provided for us through His death, burial, and resurrection.

On our website, you will find many free ministry resources and discipleship programs made available by our generous partners.

Terradez.com

Connect with Us

- ▶ **Terradez.tv**
- f **Terradez Ministries**
- ⊙ **@terradezministries**
- ⊕ **Terradez.com**
- ✉ **info@terradez.com**
- ✆ **+1 (719) 600-3344**
- ✉ **6660 Delmonico Dr. Suite D272, Colorado Springs, CO 80919**

SCAN ME

OTHER BOOKS BY TERRADEZ MINISTRIES

All Is Not Lost: *Your Path from Trauma to Victory*

Fearless: *Breaking the Habit of Fear*

Miracles and Healing Made Easy: *Inspiring Stories of Faith*

Your Life with God: *What It Means to Be Born Again and Receive the Baptism of the Holy Spirit*

39 Reasons Healing is Yours: *Healing Scriptures That Beat Sickness to Death*

Hannah and the Beanstalk! *A True Story of Faith*

Hannah and the Lost Jelly Shoe *A True Story of Faith*

Hearing God: *31 Daily Devotions That Tune You in to God's Frequency*

AVAILABLE ON OUR WEBSITE
TERRADEZ.COM/SHOP

MORE RESOURCES
BY ASHLEY TERRADEZ

GOD WANTS YOU RICH

Prosperity is one of God's most controversial promises. God Wants You Rich will show you directly from the Word of God that having wealth is not selfish and that God desires His children to prosper. Ashley addresses misconceptions and common myths about wealth in the body of Christ.

THORNS, BARNS, & OIL JARS
UPDATED & EXPANDED EDITION

In this updated edition of Thorns, Barns & Oil Jars, Ashley has added powerful additional content, and dozens of real-life testimonies, that will empower you to uproot unbiblical ideas regarding God's plan for your financial success!

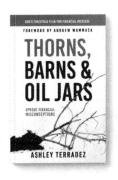

BUY, SELL, REPEAT

Got junk? In this 20-lesson course, you'll learn how to turn your "trash" into cash, even if you have never sold anything before!

BUY, RENT, REPEAT

This 10-lesson course will equip you with everything you need to know to begin a lucrative short-term rental business.

These resources are available for purchase at
Terradez.com/Shop

Did you know Terradez Ministries offers a variety of teaching, discipleship, and community resources through our website? From hours of audio and video, to teaching articles, and even an online Bible training program, there is something for everyone!

POWER ACADEMY

Our **free** online Bible school empowers believers around the globe to receive a personal revelation of God's promises and manifest them in their lives.

BOOTCAMP

We launched our Bootcamp Zoom Ministry Training Program to be a powerful discipleship opportunity. Bootcamp allows participants to connect with other believers and learn to understand and boldly share their faith.

UNDERGROUND COMMUNITY

Due to increasing censorship among secular social media platforms, we developed Underground. This safe environment empowers believers from around the world to minister to and encourage each other.

ABUNDANT LIFE TV

The Abundant Life television program is a great way to receive a short teaching to inspire you! We currently broadcast on some of the largest Christian television networks around the world. Our television archives and broadcast schedule are available on our website at Terradez.com/Today!

GLOBAL CHURCH FAMILY

Global Church Family is a group of Kingdom-minded lead pastors who are dedicated to building the local church. Through this network, we empower, build-up, and support pastors so they can make a greater impact in their communities and the world.

FREE RESOURCES

Each year, we distribute thousands of dollars' worth of books, media and confession cards around the world. Thanks to our partners, we are able to host free events and offer extensive teachings online at no cost to the viewers. You can sign up on our website to receive weekly encouraging email messages!

Check out these programs

ON OUR WEBSITE:
TERRADEZ.COM/SHOP

YOUR HOUSE OF
FAITH

Sign up for a **FREE** subscription to the
Harrison House digital magazine and get
excellent content delivered directly to your inbox!
harrisonhouse.com/signup

Sign up for Messages that Equip You to Walk in the Abundant Life

• Receive biblically sound and Spirit-filled encouragement to focus on and maintain your faith
• Grow in faith through biblical teachings, prayers, and other spiritual insights
• Connect with a community of believers who share yo values and beliefs

Experience Fresh Teachings and Inspiration to Build Your Faith

• Deepen your understanding of God's purpose for your life
• Stay connected and inspired on your faith journey
• Learn how to grow spiritually in your walk with God

In the Right Hands, This Book Will Change Lives!

Most of the people who need this message will not be looking for this book. To change their lives, you need to **put a copy of this book in their hands.**

Our ministry is constantly seeking methods to find the people who need this anointed message to change their lives. **Will you help us reach these people?**

Extend this ministry by sowing three, five, ten, or *even more* books today and change people's lives for the better! Your generosity will be part of catalyzing the Great Awakening that many have been prophesying and praying for.